Knitting
in the
Fast Lane

**Christina L. Holmes
and Mary Colucci**

Published by

krause
publications

The World's Largest Hobby & Collectibles Publisher

700 E. State St.
Iola, WI 54990-0001
Telephone 715-445-2214
www.krause.com

Please call or write for our free catalog. Our toll-free number to place an order or obtain a free catalog is 800-258-0929 or please use our regular business telephone 715-445-2214.

Library of Congress Catalog Number: 2001088099

ISBN: 0-87349-270-6

Printed in the United States of America

Creative Director: Christina L. Holmes
Technical Editor: Evie Rosen
Illustrations: Jan Wojtech

Acknowledgments

We would like to thank the knitting yarn companies who generously provided designs for this book, and the creative staff who worked with us on these projects: Sara Arblaster of Bernat Yarns; Margery Winter of Berroco, Inc.; Kathleen Sams of Coats & Clark; and Adina Klein of Lion Brand Yarns.

Special thanks also go to Anne Chua Greenwald for knitting the Weekend Chic Rollneck Pullover in a week; and to Arlene Levine for knitting the base scarf for our Loop Trim Scarf.

We'd also like to thank long-suffering husbands Irving Greenwald and Philip Weinstein, and our patient, supportive animal friends: Mary's Moustan and Christina's Shy, Mao-Me, Sir Beasley and Tony the Tiger.

A big thank-you to our wonderful models: Felicia Allen, Brett Bivona, Carole Grajek, Irving Greenwald, Michael Greenwald, Rachel Greenwald, Barry Holmes, Caitlin Holmes, "Daisy" Holmes, Lauren Holmes, Jake Levine, Shari Levine, Zachary Levine, Lisa McLaughlin, Lauren Rudman, Jeremy Weinstein, and Dolores Zipfel. Thanks too, to Colin Campbell-Harris for his lighting expertise.

Last but not least, special thanks to Evie Rosen, who has always been our favorite teacher and problem-solver, and with whose help *Knitting in the Fast Lane* stayed on track.

More about Evie...

Evie Rosen is the creator of Warm Up America!, and owned the Knitting Nook, a retail specialty store in Wausau, WI, for over 30 years. Evie is a noted knitting authority who teaches extensively for associations and professional guilds and has authored more than 25 books and leaflets, including the best-selling book, *The All New Teach Yourself to Knit*. Rosen divides her time between teaching and traveling on behalf of Warm Up America!

Evie Rosen, technical editor on this project.

Table Of Contents

Introduction

Who has time to knit? You do!

You don't have to be living in a big city to be living "in the fast lane" these days. Whether you're caught up in the electronic and digital wonders that have sped up our lives so much, or running non-stop juggling kids, work, and home, it's easy to run out of time for the things that make you feel good. Working with the wonderful texture of yarn, being creative, and making gifts that warm the heart are important things to make time for.

We feel the same way. That's why we wanted to write a book that makes knitting a bit more manageable for the fast pace of today's lifestyle. It combines fun, wearable, fashion-right designs with bulky yarns, or multi-stranding, and most are worked on larger needles. Or sometimes it's just a small-size project. Whatever it is, we want you to be able to finish it and enjoy it within a reasonable amount of time.

We don't consider ourselves "expert" knitters (we don't knit away while looking out the window and carrying on a conversation and think intricate intarsia designs are a snap). Basically, we're "average." But we really do enjoy the creativity of knitting and working with wonderful yarns. You'll find some helpful tips we've picked up along the way on working with the yarns used here, and with the help of technical editor Evie Rosen, the answers to some Frequently Asked Questions that come up when you're on a roll at 11 p.m. and have no one to call.

We've used traffic signs to draw your attention to items you might not notice if you're reading too fast, such as needle or stitch changes, or special pattern notes.

You'll find stitch instructions in the back of this book that should cover just about every stitch used in the patterns contained here, so you can have a reference guide handy instead of taking the time to look up stitches or techniques for correcting mistakes elsewhere.

We hope you'll find these designs fun to work and great to wear. So, put it in gear and start knitting!

Christina & Mary

CHAPTER 1

STARTING OUT

Welcome to *Knitting in the Fast Lane*. This book is about projects you can realistically complete without making them your life's work, depending on your skill level and the time you have available for knitting. We've tried to give you an idea of the complexity of the project in our introduction to each design, but it's all subjective, based on your skill level and what you like to do. Some designs are worked in one piece so they'll require fewer steps in assembling; others are worked in separate pieces because having it all on one needle would be much too heavy and bulky to work comfortably. In fact, most are worked on the larger-size needles.

This book is also about having some (though not all) of the answers you need in one convenient place. We have some obvious advice for getting organized (which few of us heed until we get stuck on the roadside); answers to frequently asked questions that come up from knitters of all skill levels; and stitch instructions so you don't have to search for your basic instruction book when you want to keep going on a project.

What this book is most about, however, is having fun and being creative—at your own speed.

Getting Organized

Knitting is like any other journey: You'll save a lot of time by being prepared in advance for your trip. For today's fast-lane knitters this means:

Choosing a do-able project (destination). If you're only comfortable travelling quickly on smooth roads, then stick to projects you feel you can finish realistically. This means choosing:

❖ Small projects with no fitting necessary and a minimum of finishing required;

❖ Bulky yarns or multi-stranding (two or more strands held together, which give you the option of combining different colors for tweedy or graduated color effects);

❖ Projects worked on larger needles.

For beginners, the general recommendation is to use smooth, non-textured yarns versus more highly-textured ones (although many of the new textured yarns can also be wonderfully easy to work with).

"I don't like the yarn used…" If you don't like the yarn shown in the pattern, or feel it's too expensive, buy a skein of a yarn you like and work up a gauge swatch to see if it matches and how the yarn you prefer drapes compared to that shown in the project. (Sorry, we still have to make gauge swatches in the fast lane to avoid going off the road!) *IT ALL COMES DOWN TO GAUGE AND HOW THE YARN DRAPES.* If you substitute a yarn in a different fiber, it should have the same elasticity as the original fiber used. For example, a cotton yarn will not have the elasticity of wool. Check the yardage on your substitute yarn as well, to be sure you have enough to finish the project. While we can't guarantee the same results as shown in our photos when you change yarns (and for that matter, results are subject to individual knitting quirks such as tension), you will get a good idea from a 6" x 6" gauge swatch how your new yarn works up.

*Speaking of gauge, that swatch need not be wasted. You may choose to put your gauge swatches in a notebook with notes about the pattern or use it to test-clean for washing methods. If you make a 7" X 9" swatch, you may donate it to Warm Up America!, c/o Craft Yarn Council of America, P.O. Box 9, Gastonia, NC 28053. Warm Up America! is the brainchild of Evie Rosen, our technical editor on this book. Your donated swatches are joined with others to make wonderful warm blankets that are distributed throughout the U.S. to everyone from homeless children to victims of hurricanes and fires. We work with CYCA to promote that program, and can tell you first-hand how heartwarming it is to see and hear how grateful recipients are for these warm, handmade blankets. **NOTE:** For obvious reasons, the yarn used should be washable and durable.*

Experiment with different yarns. You might want to mix a smooth yarn with a highly-textured one for an interesting effect that's still easy to handle and because it's multi-stranded, it works up quickly. Remember, you can also achieve great effects from textured or variegated-color yarns using the simplest of stitches.

"Packing" For Your Trip

Pack tools and supplies in advance. If you can't find the needles or stitch marker or crochet hook or yarn needle you need, when you need it, time will be lost, and frustration will be high. Read the list of needed materials and be sure you have the right size of everything you'll need before you want to sit down and begin the project.

When choosing your yarn, buy all the yarn you need at once. Even though there are many "no dye lot" yarns these days, it's best to have all of each color you need and from the same lot number if possible; no sense being frustrated by running out of yarn.

Planning Your Route (reading instructions)

You'd never set out on a trip without looking at the map first to review your route, would you? The same principle applies to knitting. Review the whole pattern, from start to finish. You should know where you'll be every step of the way. Trust us, it will prevent you from getting confused and angry. When you read the pattern through (and it doesn't hurt to do it more than once), you'll know what to expect. The diagrams will give you the measurements of the pieces *before* they're assembled, while the measurements shown with the sizes will show the *finished* measurements.

About Sizing...

The patterns in this book represent the talents of many different designers, so sizing will vary. To decide which size is right for you, refer to the pattern diagram, measure your own body, and even measure a sweater that has a similar silhouette and fits you well.

If you want to make the body or sleeve longer or shorter, look for the place in the pattern where the instructions say, "continue knitting in the pattern established for X number of rows or inches." That's generally a good place to increase or decrease the number of rows to adjust the fit. Check your gauge information in each pattern to determine how many rows equal an inch. For example, if you want to lengthen a sleeve from 19" to 20" and the gauge is 12 rows = 2", then add six rows to add that inch. If that's too complicated, lay your knitting on a flat, smooth surface and measure it against another sweater. Just remember to make a note of any change on the pattern and make the same change on the corresponding sleeve or sweater body. Always maintain the established stitch pattern.

Traffic Signs

Throughout the patterns in this book, you'll see traffic signs that alert you to changes or draw your attention to a special stitch or technique, or an area that needs a bit more attention. Generally, we've gone by the following guidelines:

 Read through and understand before going further.

 Special tips on working this section.

 Change here (yarns or needle sizes).

The intent is to save you time by helping prevent "wrong turns," i.e., changes you might miss if you're reading too fast.

About Gauge

Think of your gauge swatch as "stitches and rows per inch." You will have more patience for gauge than you will if you have to rip out half a sweater because the gauge is way off. Gauge is probably the single most important thing you can do to ensure the correct size of your knitted project. (And by the time you've finished complaining about it, you could have finished it!)

Using the yarn, needles and pattern stitch called for at the pattern's beginning, cast on four times the speci-

fied number of stitches per inch. For example, if 5 sts = 1", cast on 20 stitches and work in the pattern stitch for 4 inches. Your swatch *should* be 4" square.

To check your gauge, slip the work off your needle, lay it right side up on a smooth, hard surface and measure across the center. If your swatch doesn't measure exactly 4" square (or whatever size was specified for the gauge), you will have to make adjustments. If the swatch came out too small, knit another one with the next size larger needles. If it was too large, try it with the next size smaller needles. Work it out until you come as close as possible to the gauge required. While you're working on your project, measure across the width of the whole piece every 3" to be sure that your gauge hasn't changed.

Working With Specialty Yarns

Several projects in this book use very large needles and/or multi-strands of yarn, incorporate faux fur yarns, highly-textured fibers or hand-dyed yarns, any of which you may not have worked with before. Here are some tips we've picked up working on this book.

On Big Needles...

Sizes 17 and above generally come in different materials—metal alloys and plastics. Many knitters prefer the plastic needles to help control the more slippery yarns.

If you're into row counters, they won't fit on the really big needles. At one of Christina's favorite local shops, The Stitchery in Pearl River, NY, owners Judi and Adam Leber recommend using a safety pin to affix the row counter right to the garment.

Markers don't come big enough for sizes 17 and above either; the Lebers use bone rings or pieces of yarn as markers.

On Multi-Stranding...

Make believe you're working with one big strand, and hold the strands together in your hands as you would a single strand.

It's important that the different skeins you're pulling from remain untangled. This can be managed from two ends: First, keep the skeins in separate bags or baskets or whatever storage units you're using. Then, use a favorite trick from the Lebers: Depending on the thickness of your yarn, take a thread spool or a spool from an empty adding machine tape and thread the multi-strands of yarn through the spool before you cast on. The weight of the spool on the yarn will help keep the yarn manageable as you knit.

As with the faux fur yarns, this is one place where you have to keep your eyes on the road. It's easy to put your needle through the middle of a multi-strand stitch and wind up with extra stitches, so don't go into cruise control and look away too much.

On Fur & Other Novelties...

A few hints for getting the smoothest ride from some of these luxury or sporty vehicles:

❖ With any fur, hairy or highly textured yarn, watch what you are doing. Otherwise, you can easily add extra stitches or drop stitches, and take it from us, you don't want to have to rip out rows in a fur yarn. It's very difficult to pick up dropped stitches, and the long fibers in these yarns make it just about impossible to unravel.

❖ Count stitches and count rows. A good gauge swatch will be helpful here, since fur yarns tend to be stretchy. (You can use that gauge swatch to test-clean later.)

❖ Join your new ball of yarn at the beginning of a row, for ease of weaving in (and hiding) ends. (This is a good rule to follow in general.)

❖ Cast on loosely with fur yarns because there will be very little give in the cast-on row.

❖ When finishing, use a smooth yarn in a matching color for the seaming; brushing the fur gently and lightly with a hairbrush will conceal the seam if it happens to show.

❖ Don't block or steam fur yarns; it will flatten the fibers.

❖ Another general rule that applies here is to be sure to make your stitches over the full circumference (thickness) of the needle (the shaft rather than the point), for uniformity and to meet the gauge (and so you don't have to fight to get your needle in the stitch in the next row!).

❖ Don't worry about ribbon yarns twisting as you knit: *it doesn't matter*.

If you work with hand-dyed or "hand-painted" yarns, you may see a lot of variance in color between individual hanks or skeins. The designers behind the Colinette Yarns used in our Fur-Trimmed Tabard and Weekend Chic Rollneck Pullover recommend that knitters alternate two skeins throughout the knitting, alternating the skeins every other row and carrying the yarns. We have to confess, we didn't. Instead, we tried to pick colors and skeins that seemed to be even and similar in color, and we were happy with the results.

Facts About Finishing

You're almost done! When it comes to finishing, Evie Rosen, knitting teacher and knitting maven, offers some helpful hints…

Finishing Seams

Back Stitch: This is a strong, not bulky stitch that is very acceptable for shoulders and armholes. (See Stitch Instructions for the technique in Diagram 53.)

Mattress Stitch: This is a perfect stitch for side seams and sleeve seams, and is also called Vertical Weaving or Invisible Stitch. You work under a bar between the first and second stitches on each side, alternating sides. (See Stitch Instructions for the technique.)

Three Needle Bind-Off: This is used as a shoulder bind off and shoulder seam. Hold the right sides together with knitting needles pointing in the same direction. With a third knitting needle, knit one stitch from the front needle and one from the back needle together and move the new stitch to the third needle. Knit the next two stitches together and move to the third needle. Lift the first stitch on the third needle over the second stitch to bind it off. Continue in this manner and binding off across the row. Fasten off.

Blocking

Blocking will even out your stitches, flatten your seams and give your garment a more finished, professional appearance.

Wet Blocking: If the garment is machine washable, wash it in the machine and machine dry according to manufacturer's directions on the yarn label. Otherwise, hand wash it carefully, pressing as much moisture out of it as you can. Then put it in the last four minutes of the spin cycle in your washer to remove the rest of the water. Spread on bath towels to desired size, shaping with your hands, and let it dry, checking it often for size. You may pin it to size if desired, using rust-free pins.

Steam: This will be easier with a wool yarn. Keeping the iron (or steamer) at least a half inch above the garment, steam the entire garment on the wrong side. Acrylics should only be steamed (or wet-blocked), not pressed. You can change a garment's size slightly when it is damp from the steam. Let it dry before moving it.

Pattern Coding

The introduction to each project provides an overview of the pattern instructions. In addition, we have added a coding system more detailed than the usual Easy/Intermediate/Advanced ratings, which defines the quickest and easiest patterns as Beginner1, 2 and 3, followed by Intermediate and finally, Experienced.

Beginner1, for instance, is a good first-time project with no shaping and garter and stockinette stitches.

Beginner2 projects also have simple shapes and stitches, but involve changing yarn colors and working with very textured or multiple strands of yarn, simple increases and decreases and stitch holders.

Beginner3 projects still feature simple shapes, and may use textured yarn or multiple strands, and can introduce different stitch combinations, circular needles, decreasing, increasing, and picking up stitches.

CHApTER 2

Quick Trips

Speedy Girl's Poncho

Designed by Lion Brand Yarn Co.

It's fun, fashion and easy to wear. And you'll be cruising in the fast lane with this design: one rectangle, one seam and steam—you're done!

Sizes:

Girl's sizes 4/6 (6/8, 10/12)
Block to 11 x 30" (13 x 32", 15 x 34") or as desired

Gauge:

In pattern on size 13 needles, 3 sts = 1"
To ensure proper fit, take time to check gauge.

Instructions:

Row 1: Slip 1, *k2, p2; repeat from *, end k3.
Row 2: Slip 1, *p2, k2; rep from *, end p2, k1.
Repeat rows 1 and 2 for pattern.

Cast on 32 (40, 44) sts. Work in pattern, beginning with Row 1 for 30 (32, 34)". Bind off.

Finishing:

Block. Sew bound off edge to the first 11 (13, 15)" of side edge as pictured.

MATERIALS:

❖ Lion Brand *Woolspun*
 (wool/acrylic/polyester, 100 yd) skein
 Raspberry (#112)—2 (2, 3) skeins

❖ Size 13 knitting needles or size needed to obtain gauge

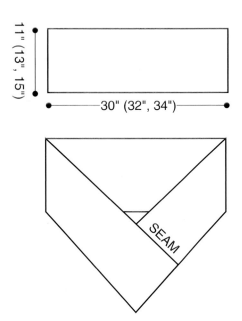

Photo: Christina L. Holmes

Sleeveless High Neck

Designed by Lion Brand Yarn Co.

This easy-to-wear design is fashion-right and fast—a straight road to style! Worked on size 13 needles, the thick-and-thin yarn makes this a quick but interesting trip.

Sizes:

Directions are for women's sizes Small
   (Medium, Large, X-Large)
Finished garment at chest measures 36 (38, 40, 42)"

Gauge:

In Stockinette stitch on size 13 needles,
   5 sts and 7 rows = 2"
To ensure the proper size, be sure to check your gauge.

Instructions:

Back

With size 13 straight needles cast on 48 (50, 52, 54) sts. Work in k1, p1 rib for 6 rows. Continue in St st until piece measures 14" from beginning, end by doing WS row.

Armhole Shaping

Bind off 3 sts at beginning of next 2 rows. Decrease row (RS): Slip 1 st, p1, k1, p1, k2tog, knit to last 6 sts, ssk, p1, k1, p1, k1. In all WS rows slip 1st st, k1, p1, k1, purl to last 4 sts, k1, p1, k1, p1. Repeat decreases one more time, 38 (40, 42, 44) sts. Work as following: (RS) slip first st, p1, k1, p1 to last 4 sts, p1, k1, p1, k1; (WS) slip first st, k1, p1, k1, purl to last 4 sts, k1, p1, k1, p1. Repeat these 2 rows until armhole measures 7 (8, 8, 9)". Bind off 10 (11, 12, 12) sts at beginning of next 2 rows. Place remaining 18 (18, 18, 20) sts onto stitch holder for back neck.

MATERIALS:

❖ Lion Brand *Woolspun*
   (wool/acrylic/polyester, 100 yd skein)
   Sky Blue (#106)—4, (4, 5, 5) skeins

❖ Size 13 (9 mm) straight knitting needles

❖ Size 13 (9 mm) 16" (40 cm) circular needles, or size needed to obtain the correct gauge

❖ 2 Stitch holders

❖ Yarn or tapestry needle for weaving in ends

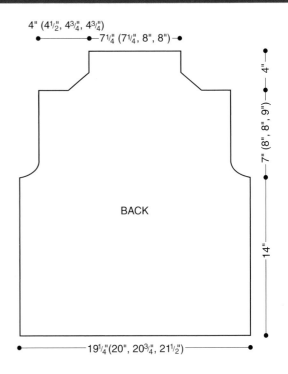

4" (4½", 4¾", 4¾")
7¼" (7¼", 8", 8")
4"
7 (8", 8", 9")
BACK
14"
19¼"(20", 20¾", 21½")

Front

Work as for back until armhole measures 5 (6, 6, 7)".

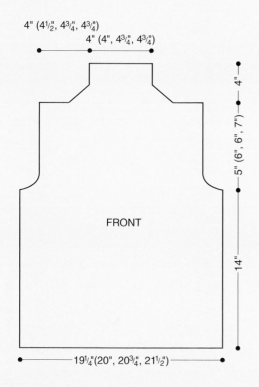

4" (4½", 4¾", 4¾")

4" (4", 4¾", 4¾")

FRONT

5" (6", 6", 7")

4"

14"

19¼"(20", 20¾", 21½")

Front Neckline Shaping

Slip 1, p1, k1, p1, k7 (8, 8, 9), ssk, k1, place next 10 (10, 12, 12) sts onto stitch holder. Attach a separate strand of yarn to other side and work remaining sts as following: k1, k2tog, k7 (8, 8, 9), p1, k1, p1, k1. Working both shoulders at the same time, repeat decreases every other row 3 more times. When front measures same as back, bind off 10 (11, 12, 12) sts from each shoulder edge.

Neck

Sew shoulders together. With RS facing and circular needle, work across 18 (18, 18, 20) sts from Back holder, pick up 5 sts on left side of neck, work across 10 (10, 12, 12) sts from front holder, pick up 5 sts on the right side of the neck—38 (38, 42, 42) sts. Next round: Work in k1, p1. Work around until neckband measures 4". Bind off loosely.

Finishing:

Sew side seams. Weave ends. Block.

Photo: Christina L. Holmes

Quick Cropped Top

Designed by Elena Malo

Simply stylish, this flattering, capped-sleeve top is made in one piece on size 11 needles. Be sure to use a soft yarn as shown, so the top drapes properly.

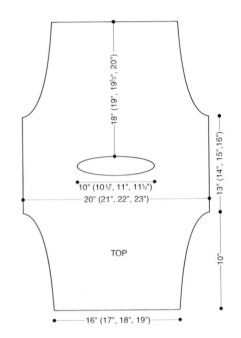

Sizes:

Directions are for women's sizes Small (Medium, Large, X-Large)
Finished garment at chest measures 36 (38, 40, 42)"

Gauge:

In Stockinette stitch on size 11 needles, 3 sts and 4 rows = 1 "
To ensure proper fit, take time to check the gauge.

Instructions:

 Top is made in one piece, beginning at lower back edge.

With size 11 straight needles, cast on 48 (51, 54, 57) sts. Work in St st for 10 rows. Increase 1 st each side, repeat increase every 10 rows, 2 more times. Repeat increase every other row 3 times, 60 (63, 66, 69) sts. Work until piece measures 18 (19, 19½, 20)".

Neckline

Work over first 15 (16, 18, 19) sts. Bind off next 30 (31, 30, 31) sts, work to end of row. Next row work first 15 (16, 18, 19) sts, cast on 30 (31, 30, 31) sts, work to end of row. Continue even on 60 (63, 66, 69) sts until piece measures 6 (6½, 7, 7½)" from neckline cast on. Decrease 1 st each side every other row 3 times. Work 10 rows. Repeat decrease. Repeat decrease every 10 rows, 2 more times. Work 10 rows, bind off with a knit row on WS.

Finishing:

Holding work RS up, with circular needle pick up 60 (63, 60, 62) sts around neckline. Bind off with a knit row from WS.
Sew side seams. With circular needle repeat this same finishing around each armhole picking up 30 (42, 45, 48) sts and around lower edge, picking up 96 (102, 108, 114). Finish off all ends.

MATERIALS:

❖ Berroco, *Pronto*
     (cotton/acrylic, 55 yds/50 gm ball)
     So Blue #4450—7 balls

❖ Size 11 straight needles, or needle
     size to obtain gauge

❖ Size 11 circular needle—16"
     (for finishing)

❖ Yarn or tapestry needle for finishing

Photo: Christina L. Holmes

Plushest Pullover

Designed by Elena Malo

Picture a luxurious limo—this is the softest ride imaginable, and lightweight too! Knit mostly on size 15 needles using two strands, with the body made in one piece, this is a loose-fitting design everyone can wear.

Sizes:

Directions are for women's sizes Small
   (Medium, Large, X-Large)
Finished garment at chest measures 36 (40, 44, 48)"

Gauge:

In Stockinette stitch, using 2 strands of Plush and
   size 15 needles, 8 sts and 12 rows = 4".
To ensure proper fit, take time to check the gauge.

Instructions:

▽ Sweater is knit in the round, using circular needles. See page 126 for information on working with circular needles.

Body

With longer circular needles size 13 and A, cast on 72 (80, 88, 96) sts. Work in rounds in k1, p1 ribbing for 3 rows.
   ▽ (Place a marker at the end of first row, to help you determine when you are about to begin a new row.)
   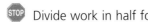 Change to circular needles size 15 and 2 strands of MC. Knit all rows until piece measures 14" from start.

🛑 Divide work in half for back and front.

Back

Work over 36 (40, 44, 48) sts, place remaining sts on holder. Work in St st until piece measures 7½ (8, 8½, 9)".
   Place first 12 (14, 15, 17) sts on a holder for left shoulder, center 12 (12, 14, 14) sts on a separate holder for back neckline, last 12 (14, 15, 17) sts for right shoulder.

MATERIALS:

❖ Berroco *Plush* (acrylic, 90 yds/50 gm ball) Java Purple (#1916)—10 (10, 12, 12) balls—Main Color (MC)

❖ Berroco *X-Press* (wool/acrylic, 42 yds/ 50 gm balls) Java Plum—2 balls—Color A

❖ Size 13 circular needle—16"

❖ Size 13 circular needles—24"

❖ Size 15 circular needle—24" or size to obtain gauge

❖ 6 stitch holders

❖ Yarn or tapestry needle for finishing

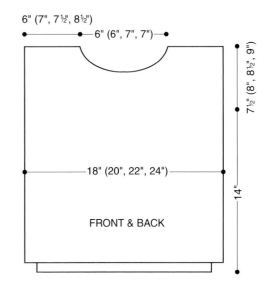

6" (7", 7½", 8½")

6" (6", 7", 7")

7½" (8", 8½", 9")

18" (20", 22", 24")

14"

FRONT & BACK

Front

Pick up remaining sts. Join 2 new strands of MC, work in St st until piece measures 6 (6, 6½, 6½)".

Neckline Shaping

Work over first 15 (17, 18, 20) sts, leave next 6 (6, 8, 8) sts on holder. Join 2 new strands of MC, work each shoulder separately. Bind off 2 sts at neck edge once, decrease 1 st once. Work even until front corresponds to back. Place remaining 12 (14, 15, 17) sts of each shoulder on holders.

Sleeves

Make 2. With size 13 needles (short circulars) and A, cast on 23 (23, 25, 27) sts. Work in rounds in k1 p1 ribbing for 3 rows.

Change to size 15 needles and 2 strands of MC, work in St st for 8 rows. Increase 1 st each end. Repeat increase every 8th row 4 (5, 5, 5) times; 33 (35, 37, 39) sts. Work even until piece measures 19" from the beginning. Bind off.

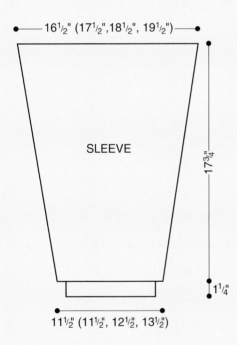

16½" (17½", 18½", 19½")

SLEEVE

17¾"

1¼"

11½" (11½", 12½", 13½")

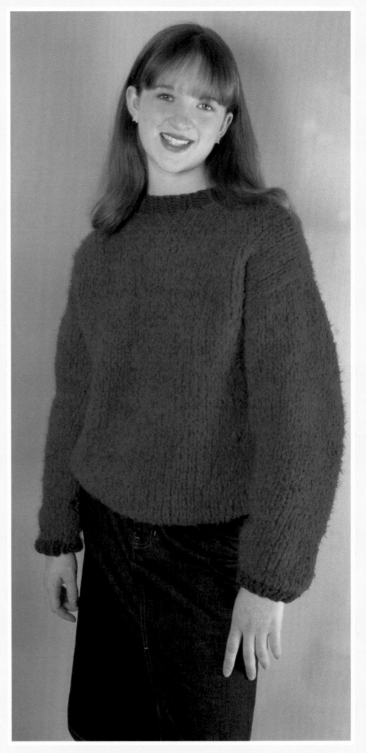

Photo: Christina L. Holmes

Finishing:

STOP Three-needle finishing: Place front and back shoulder sts on 2 separate needles (13 and 15 circulars). Holding work with WS together, with a third size 13 needle, *knit 1 st from front and 1 from back together.* Repeat from * 1 more time and bind off first st. Repeat across. Repeat for other shoulder.

With the RS of the sweater facing you, using size 13 needles (short circular) and color A, pick up 34 (36, 36, 38) sts around neckline. Work 5 rows in k1, p1 ribbing. Bind off in ribbing loosely. Pin sleeves to armholes and sew together using backstitch. Sew sleeve seams.

Fringed Necklace & Beaded Necklace

Designed by Arnetta Kenney

Depending on the yarn and beads you choose, these little necklaces can have the fashionable look of the 1970s or be elegantly Victorian. Beads are added to the fringe or threaded onto the yarn in advance and later knitted into the stitches.

Gauge:

In garter stitch and size 6 needles, 23 sts = 4"
To ensure proper fit, take time to check gauge.

Instructions:

Using 1 strand cast on 3 sts.
Row 1: K1, yo, k1, yo, end k1.
Row 2: K1, yo, k to end of row—6 sts.
Row 3: K1, yo, k to last st, yo, k1—8 sts.
Row 4: K.
Repeat rows 3 & 4 until there are a total of 22 sts, end with Row 4.
🛑 To create the straps for the necklace, you will cast on stitches at end of Row 4, which is one of the top corners of the necklace triangle. Then you will knit across these new stitches, continuing knitting across the necklace and then at the other top corner, cast on stitches for the second strap.

> ### FRINGED NECKLACE MATERIALS:
>
> - J & P Coats *Speed–Cro–Sheen* (cotton, 100 yd ball) Size 3 Vanilla (#007)—1 ball
>
> - 1 large center bead
>
> - 12 medium-to-large beads for fringe
>
> - 1 small-to-medium button for necklace closure
>
> - Size 6 needle (or size needed to obtain gauge)
>
> - Needle for threading beads

Necklace Strap

Row 1: At the end of Row 4, cast on 32 sts, by knitting into the end stitch, and placing the newly formed st onto the left needle 🛑 Do not remove old st from left needle.) Continue adding new sts, until you have cast on 32 new sts.
▽ Strap length is approximately 6½". Adjust length as desired by increasing or decreasing the number of stitches you cast on.

Row 2: K into the back loop of the new 32 sts. Work the 22 necklace sts in pattern established: K1, yo, knit to last st, yo, k1. Following instructions as in row 1, cast on 32 sts creating the second strap.

Row 3: K into the back loop of the new 32 sts. K the 22 necklace sts in pattern established and k the sts of the first strap.

Row 4-6: K every st, yo above previous yarn overs every other row.

Row 7: Bind off across row.

Finishing:

To make the necklace fringe, cut 18, 12" lengths of yarn. (Two lengths per fringe.)

Loop one set of fringe through the eyelet hole at the center bottom. Loop the remaining fringe through the eyelet holes along side edges of necklace. There should be 4 strands in each fringe.

STOP To make twisted fringe: Separate each fringe into 2 groups (2 strands per group), twist each group to the right tightly, while twisted place both groups together then twist in the opposite direction (to the left). While maintaining twist, thread a bead(s) onto twisted fringe, then knot the twisted fringe closely to bead. Repeat with other fringe. For a graduated look, cut each fringe shorter than the bottom one.

▽ Making twisted cord can be tricky, especially when you are twisting two threads. It's helpful to place the necklace on a hard, flat surface, twist one set of threads tightly, tape the ends to the surface with regular adhesive tape so they can't unravel, and then twist the second set of threads. To twist the two sides of fringe together, it's helpful to hold the two sides together with one hand and twist with the other. Experiment with bead placement and the number of beads.

Sew a loop to the back of one strap and add a button to the other.

Gauge:

In garter stitch, 23 sts = 4"
To ensure proper fit, take time to check gauge.

Instructions:

STOP Thread 10 beads onto the yarn before you begin. Beads will be held behind your knitting and when you are ready to position them on the necklace, you simply pull the bead up to your needles.

Using 1 strand, cast on 3 sts. Follow Fringed Necklace pattern, positioning the beads where desired on the necklace triangle. **STOP** To position the bead, bring the bead forward, close to work, slip the next st (bead sits in front of this stitch), knit next stitch. Knit the slipped stitch on the next row. Continue following the Fringed Necklace pattern until there are a total of 22 sts, ending with Row 4.

Necklace Strap

Continue to follow pattern for Fringed Necklace, binding off on Row 6.

Finishing:

Sew beads onto necklace edge, just below eyelet holes. Sew a loop at end of one strap and button at the end of the other.

BEADED NECKLACE MATERIALS:

❖ J & P Coats® *"Speed–Cro–Sheen"* (cotton, 100 yd ball) Size 3 Navy (#486)—1 ball

❖ 10 medium-to-large beads

❖ 1 small-to-medium button for necklace closure

❖ Size 6 needle, or size needed to obtain gauge

❖ Needle for threading beads

Chapter 3

Country Weekend

Fur-Trimmed Tabard & Cowl

Designed by Elena Malo

From Aspen to Zermatt, this chic tabard in hand-dyed yarn with faux fur trim would look great wherever you are! Worked on size 15 needles for speed, and secured with twisted ties on each side for adjustable fit. With the option of a separate "fur" cowl and ski band, you'll be fashionably warm.

Sizes:

Womens sizes Small (Medium, Large, X-Large)
Finished chest size, 40 (44, 48, 52)"

Gauge:

In Stockinette stitch, using *Point Five* yarn and size 15 needles,
   11 sts and 15 rows = 5"
To ensure the proper size, take time to check your gauge.

Tabard Instructions:

Back

With straight needles and A, cast on 42 (46, 51, 55) sts. Knit for 3 rows, ending with WS row. Work in St st; for selvedge slip first st of every row. Work until piece measures 24". Work first 13 (15, 17, 19) sts and place on holder, bind off next 16 (16, 17, 17) sts for the back of the neck, place remaining 13 (15, 17, 19) sts on a stitch holder for left shoulder.

MATERIALS:

❖ Colinette Hand-Dyed *Point Five* (wool, 54 yds/100 gm hank) Summer Berries (#109)
   Color A—6 (6, 7, 7) hanks

❖ Mondial *Fur* (wool/acrylic/polyester, 50 gm hank/49 yds) (color #85)
   Color B—4 hanks
NOTE: This is sufficient yarn to trim tabard and complete cowl and ski band.

❖ Size 15 straight needles, or size to obtain gauge

❖ Size 15 circular needles, 24" long (for finishing)

❖ 4 stitch holders

Photo: Christina L. Holmes

Front

Work the same as for back until 21½" from beginning, end with WS row.

Neckline Shape and Shoulders

K first 17 (19, 21, 23) sts. Place remaining sts on holder. Row 1: Bind off first 2 sts, p to end. Row 2-4: K to last 3 sts, slip 1, k1, psso (pass slip stitch over knit stitch), k1. Work on remaining 13 (15, 17, 19) sts until front measures the same as back. Place stitches on holder.
Pick up sts on holder. Join A, bind off next 8 (8, 9, 9) sts and k to end of row. Work on remaining 17 (19, 21, 23) sts. Shape right shoulder as for left but reverse shaping. Place stitches on holder.

Finishing:

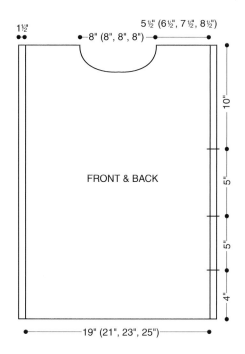

▽ Following is an alternate method of joining seams which is called three-needle bind off. It is the neatest finish for shoulder seams. As its name suggests, you use three needles. Try this or you can bind off the shoulder stitches and join the shoulder seams using backstitch. Place front and back shoulder sts on separate needles. Holding work with RS facing, with another size 15 needle, knit 1 st from front and 1 st from back together and at the same time, bind off. Repeat on other shoulder.

Finish Side Edge: With RS facing, size 15 circular needles and 2 strands of B, pick up the first st (selvedge stitch) every 2nd row, from beginning of back to beginning of front. Work in St st for 3 rows, bind off on 4th row loosely.

Side Ties

There are six, 12" long twisted-cord ties on each side of the tabard, approximately 5" apart. (See illustration for exact placement.) Each tie is made by twisting four strands of yarn.

Cut 24, 36" long strands of color A. For each tie, hold together two strands, fold them in half and draw the loop end through the side edge of the tabard, at the designated point. Using your fingers or a crochet hook, draw the ends through the loop to secure the tie just as you would if you were making a fringe. Take two of the four strands and twist them to the right. Secure them so they do not unravel and take the second two strands and twist them to the right. Then hold the two twisted cords together and twist them tightly to the left. Make a knot at the end and trim close to the knot. Finished cord will measure approximately 12" long.

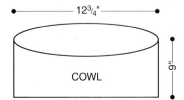

Detachable Cowl

With circular needles and 2 strands of B, cast on 36 sts. Work in rounds, knit each round, until piece measures 9". Bind off very loosely. Fasten off and weave in all ends.

Fur Ski Band

Designed by Christina L. Holmes

This is a real downhill racer! Worked in two strands of *Fur*, knit stitch all the way, it's fast and easy. (You can also use this basic pattern to make a man's ski band in another, more masculine yarn. Guys whose occupation demands they work outside in the cold weather especially appreciate these in bright, neon colors that motorists can see.)

Size:

Measure the head you want to fit. Keep in mind that this is worked in knit stitches in a "stretchy" direction, so you'll want to make it a little snug to allow for stretch (about an inch smaller than the head size). Ours measures 3" x 22½".

Instructions:

Working with two strands of *Fur* yarn on size 15 needles, cast on 7 stitches. Knit until piece measures 22½" long (or size desired). Bind off, leaving a 12" tail of yarn for seaming. Try on the band for fit, and seam as desired, using overcast stitch.

3"
SKIBAND
22½"

Silvery "Shearling" Vest & Hat

Designed by Lion Brand Yarn Co.

We love the look of shearling—why not knit it? The vest is made in one piece, with a single strand of this bulky chenille on size 10½ needles. The "fur" yarn is worked with two strands held together on size 7 needles. Be sure to measure for the head size on the hat, which is sized for a generous fit; some may prefer a more snug fit.

Sizes:

Women's sizing Small (Medium, Large, Extra Large)
Finished chest measurement: 36 (39, 42, 46)"

Gauge:

With *Chenille* yarn on size 10½ needles in Stockinette stitch,
    2½ sts and 3 rows = 1"
With *daVinci* yarn on size 7 needles in Stockinette stitch with two
    strands of yarn held together, 4½ sts and 6 rows = 1"
To ensure proper fit, take time to check your gauge.

Instructions:

Vest Back & Front (knit in one continuous piece)

With single strand of *Chenille* and size 10½ needles, cast on 45 (49, 53, 58) sts. Work in St st for 18 (18½, 18½, 19)".
▽ Make length adjustments at this point. ◇CAUTION◇ Work one row of Reverse St st, then continue working in St st until piece measures 24½ (25, 25½, 26)" from start.

Neck Shaping

Work 13 (14, 16, 18) sts, bind off center 19 (21, 21, 22) sts. Join a second ball of yarn and work remaining 13 (14, 16, 18) sts.

MATERIALS:

❖ Lion Brand *Chenille "Thick & Quick®"* (acrylic/rayon, 100yd skein) grey (#149)
Vest (all sizes)—4 skeins
Hat (all sizes)—1 skein

❖ Lion Brand *daVinci* (nylon, 1¾ oz/50 gm/121 yd ball) Marble (#152) for faux fur trim
Vest (all sizes)—2 skeins
Hat (all sizes)—1 skein

❖ Worsted-weight yarn—a small quantity of grey (approximately 6 yards) for finishing seams (See finishing notes in the pattern.)

❖ Size 10½/6.5mm circular needles, or size to obtain gauge

❖ Size 7/4.5mm circular needles

❖ Size 9/5.5mm circular needles

❖ Size H/8 crochet hook

❖ 7 fur hook closures

❖ Yarn or tapestry needle for finishing

❖ Yarn markers

Photo: Christina L. Holmes

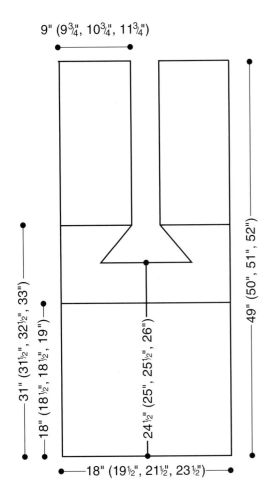

9" (9¾", 10¾", 11¾")

49" (50", 51", 52")

31" (31½", 32½", 33")

18" (18½", 18½", 19")

24½" (25", 25½", 26")

18" (19½", 21½", 23½")

Working both sides at once, work even for 2 rows. Increase 1 st at neck edge every other row 9 (10, 10, 11) times, 22 (24, 26, 29) sts, and at same time when piece measures 31 (31½, 32½, 33)" from start work, 1 row of Reverse St st. Continue working in St st until piece measures 49 (50, 51, 52)" from start. Bind off all sts.

Finishing:

Sew side seams. ▽ Chenille is difficult to sew with. We recommend weaving together the side seams using a similar color of a worsted-weight yarn.

Front Faux Fur Edging

With size 7 needles and two strands of *daVinci* faux fur yarn, pick up 70 (70, 72, 72) sts along one of the front edges from bottom of piece to start of neck shaping. Work in Reverse St st (so that the fur rolls inward toward the WS of the sweater) for 6 rows. Bind off all sts with size 10½ needles. Repeat pattern on the other front edge.

Neck Edging

With a size 7 needle and a double strand of *daVinci* faux fur yarn, pick up 72 (74, 81, 83) sts around neck edge starting at neck shaping. Work in garter stitch for 9 rows.

 Bind off all sts with size 10½ needles.

Bottom Edging

With RS facing, size 7 needles and two strands of *daVinci* "fur" yarn, pick up 153 (171, 189, 207) sts along bottom edge. Work in St st (so that the fur rolls outward toward the right side of the sweater) for 6 rows. Bind off all sts with size 10½ needles.

Armhole Edging

With RS facing, size 7 needles and a double strand of daVinci "fur" yarn, pick up 90 (100, 102, 104) sts around armhole edge. Work in St st (so that the fur rolls outward toward the right side of the sweater) for 6 rows. Bind off all sts with size 10½ needles.

Yoke "Seams"

With size 7 needles and two strands of *daVinci* "fur" yarn, pick up 38 (43, 47, 51) sts along Reverse St st yoke ridge along each front. Work in garter st for 2 rows. Bind off all sts with size 10½ needles. Again, using size 7 needles, pick up 77 (85, 95, 103) sts along Reverse St st ridge at back yoke, and work in garter st for 2 rows. Bind off all sts with size 10½ needles.

Sew 7 fur hooks and loops along the front opening, spaced evenly from bottom of vest to start of neck opening.

Hat (generous sizing):

With size 10½ needles and one strand of *Chenille Thick & Quick*, cast on 4 sts. Working in St st, increase 1 st into each stitch (8 sts). Next row: Purl. Next row: Knit all sts, increase 1 st into every other stitch (12 sts). Continue working in St st, placing a marker every 3 sts (4 markers total). Increase 1 st before each marker every other round until there are 13 sts between each marker, 52 sts total. Work even until piece measures 7". ⬦ Switch to size 9 circular needles and continue working in St st until piece measures 9½". ⬦ With two strands of *daVinci* "fur" yarn and size 7 circular needles, k1, increase 1 st into each stitch across the row, k1 (102 sts). Work in St st for 2½". ⬦ Bind off all sts with size 10½ needles.

Finishing:

▽ **NOTE:** Sizing adjustments can be made when you are finishing the hat. For instance, before sewing the hat seam, pin it and try it on to make sure you like the fit. Do the same thing before you fold and stitch the fur trim cuff.

Sew hat seam. Turn up bottom 5". At the point where the fur trim starts, tack cuff to the hat all the way around. Turn down fur so that it completely covers cuff. With a double strand of fur and a yarn or tapestry needle whipstitch the bottom of the fur trim to the bottom of the cuff, securing it all the way around the hat.

Lay hat flat. Make a faux fur "seam" with a double strand of *daVinci* yarn and a size H crochet hook. Work one row of single crochet beginning from the fur cuff, along the diameter of the hat dome to the opposite side of the cuff. Lay hat flat so that fur seam is in the direct center of the hat and make a second faux seam perpendicular to the first so that both seams intersect at the hat's tip.

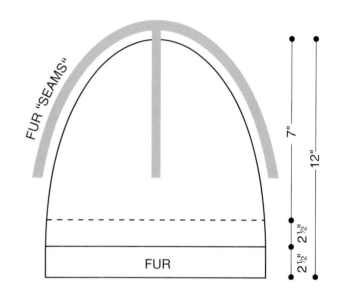

Sporty Slip-Stitch Turtleneck

Designed by Brenda A. Lewis for Coats & Clark

Three strands held together make a cozy, oversized turtleneck that's easy to wear. The pattern stitch creates a woven look, but you won't have to do any weaving on this one. Try out the pattern stitch first, by making a swatch, and it will be a much easier project.

Sizes:

Directions are for women's sizes Small (Medium, Large)
Finished chest size: 40 (44, 48)"
Sleeve length: 19 (20, 21)"

Gauge:

In pattern stitch with size 17 needles, 12 sts
  and 18 rows = 4".
To ensure the proper fit, take time to check your gauge.
NOTE: Hold 3 strands together throughout.

Pattern Stitch:

Row 1: Using 17 needles and MC knit.
Row 2: MC purl.
Row 3: CC k1, *slip 1 purlwise, k1, repeat from *.
Row 4: CC k1, *(yarn forward, slip 1 purlwise, yarn back), k1 repeat from *.
Rows 5 & 6: As rows 1 & 2.
Rows 7 & 8: As rows 3 & 4.
Rows 9 & 10: As rows 1 & 2.
Rows 11 & 12: ⬦CAUTION⬦ Using **MC** as rows 3 & 4.
Rows 13 & 14: As rows 1 & 2.
Rows 15 & 16: As rows 3 & 4.
Rows 17 & 18: As rows 1 & 2.
Rows 19 & 20: As rows 11 & 12.

MATERIALS:

❖ Red Heart® *Soft* (Bounce-Back® acrylic, 5 oz/328 yd skein)
  Light Yellow Green (#7672), Main Color (MC)—7 (7, 9) skeins
  Dark Yellow Green (#7675), Contrasting Color (CC)—2 skeins

❖ Size 11/8mm knitting needles

❖ Size 17/12.75mm knitting needles, or size needed to obtain gauge

❖ Size 10 circular knitting needles, 16"

❖ Yarn or tapestry needle for finishing

❖ 3 stitch holders

Photo: Mary Colucci

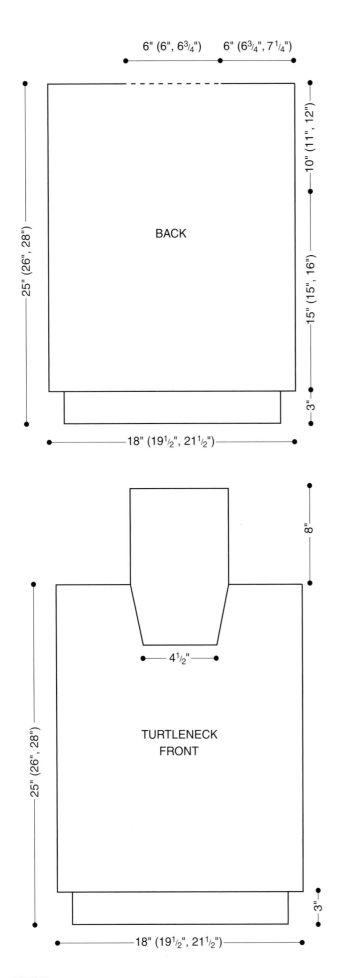

Instructions:

Back

Using size 11 needles and MC cast on 45 (49, 53) sts. Work k1, p1 ribbing for 3" ending with WS row. Repeat rows 1–20 for pattern and work in established pattern until back measures 25 (26, 28)" ending with a WS row. Bind off 15 (17, 18) sts at the beginning of each of the next 2 rows. Slip remaining 15 (15, 17) sts onto holder for neck back.

Front

Work the same as back until front measures 22 (23, 25)", ending with a WS row.

Neck Shaping

Next row work 17 (19, 21) sts in established pattern for left shoulder, slip next 11 (11, 11) sts onto holder for front neck, slip next 17 (19, 21) sts onto holder for the right shoulder. Work shoulder in established pattern and decrease 1 st at the neck edge every RS row 2 (2, 3) times. Work even until front measures 25 (26, 28)", ending with WS row. Bind off. With RS facing, leave center 11 sts on a holder, join yarn to remaining sts. Complete to correspond to first side, reversing shaping.

Sleeves

With size 10 circular needle and MC cast on 25 (25, 29) sts. Work k1, p1 ribbing for 3" ending with a WS row. 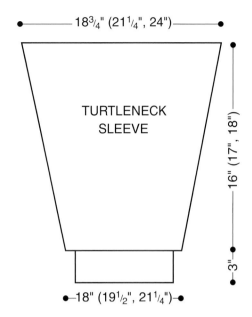 Change to size 17 needle, knit next row, increasing 6 sts evenly spaced across row. (Counts as row 1 of pattern.) Continue to work in pattern and increase 1 st each end of needle every 6th row until there are 45 (47, 53) sts. Work even in established pattern until sleeve measures 19 (20, 21)", ending with WS row. Bind off.

Finishing:

Sew shoulder seams.

Turtleneck

With size 10 circular needles, RS facing and MC, knit the 15 (15, 17) sts from holder for back neck. Pick up and knit 10 sts along side edge of neck, knit the 11 sts from holder for front neck, pick up and knit 10 sts along side edge. Place marker on needle. Work k1, p1 ribbing in rounds until neck measures 8".

▽ Bind off **loosely** in ribbing.

Measure down 10 (11, 12)" from each side of the shoulder seam and place a marker. Mark the center of the sleeve's top. Matching center of the sleeve top to shoulder seam, sew sleeve between markers.

Sew sleeve and side seam. Weave in yarn ends.

TURTLENECK SLEEVE

18³/₄" (21¹/₄", 24")

16" (17", 18")

3"

18" (19¹/₂", 21¹/₄")

Closeup of pattern stitch, right side.

Tunic With Optional Cowl

Designed by Elena Malo

We like the look of tunics as an elongated alternative to vests, and a separate cowl neck lets you add warmth and a fashion touch. Those who don't like something around their neck can go with this easy-to-wear tunic on its own. The yarn is bulky enough to use single stranded on size 13 needles and still move quickly.

Sizes:

Women's Small (Medium, Large, Extra Large)
Finished garment at chest measures 36 (40, 44, 48)"

Gauge:

On size 13 needles in Stockinette stitch, 13 sts and 7 rows = 5"
To ensure the proper size, take time to check your gauge.

MATERIALS:

❖ Reynolds *Bulky Lopi* (wool, 100gms/ 66 yd ball)—7 skeins

❖ Size 13/9mm straight needles, or size to obtain gauge

❖ Size 13/9mm circular needles, 16"

❖ 4 stitch holders

❖ Yarn or tapestry needle for finishing

Instructions:

Back

With straight needles, cast on 52 (56, 62, 66) sts. Work even in St st until piece measures 16" from start.

Armholes

Bind off 2 sts at the beginning of next 2 rows. Decrease 1 st each side as follows: K1, k2tog, work to last 3 sts, ssk (slip, slip, knit), k1. Purl one row repeat decrease row one more time. Work even until 8 (8½, 9, 9½)" from start of armhole. Place first 11 (13, 15, 17) sts on holder for left shoulder, bind off next 22 (22, 24, 24) sts for back neckline, place remaining 11 (13, 15, 17) sts on holder for right shoulder.

Front

Work same as for back to 6 (6, 6½, 6½)" from beginning of armholes.

Neck Shaping

Work over first 17 (19, 21, 23) sts, place center 10 (10, 12, 12) sts on holder. Join a second ball and knit over last 17 (19, 21, 23) sts. Work each shoulder separately. Bind off at each neck edge 3 sts once, 2 sts once, decrease 1 st each side of neckline once. Work until front length corresponds to back.

Finishing:

▽ Following is an alternate method of joining seams which is called three-needle bind off. It is the neatest finish for shoulder seams. As its name suggests, you use three needles. Try it or you can use the more common weaving (invisible) method.

Place front and back shoulder sts each on separate needles. Holding work with RS together, with another size 13 needle, knit 1 st from front needle and 1 from back needle together and at the same time, bind off. Repeat for other shoulder. Sew side seams.

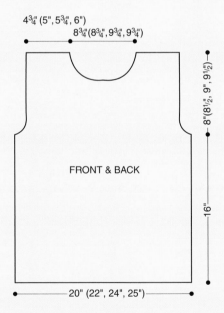

4³⁄₄" (5", 5³⁄₄", 6")
8³⁄₄" (8³⁄₄", 9³⁄₄", 9³⁄₄")
8" (8¹⁄₂", 9", 9¹⁄₂")

FRONT & BACK

16"

20" (22", 24", 25")

Photo: Christina L. Holmes

Cowl Neck Piece

With circular needles, cast on 66 sts. Work in the round in St st (knit all rows) for 9". Bind off loosely on a purl row.

▽ This can be done on straight needles and seamed (short edges) on wrong sides.

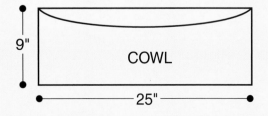

9"

COWL

25"

Weekend Chic Pullover

Designed by Evie Rosen

For those who like a little closer silhouette, this simple roll-neck pullover is a great option for day or relaxed evening, and the hand-dyed yarn revs up the style. Worked on size 17 needles, with some shaping and set-in sleeves, you also can choose to finish this with a jewel-neck collar if you prefer.

Sizes:

Women's sizes Small (Medium, Large, Extra Large)
Finished chest size 36 (40, 44, 48)"

Gauge:

On #17 needles in Stockinette stitch, 2 sts = 1"
To ensure the proper fit, take time to check gauge.

Instructions:

Back

Cast on 40 (44, 48, 52) stitches. Working in St st, decrease 1 st each end, every 1", 3 times. Continue in St st to 3½" from beginning. Next row, increase 1 st each end every 1", 3 times, then work even until piece measures 17" from the beginning. ▽ (Because of the slightly fitted style of this pattern, you might wish to adjust the length of the sweater body. Just remember, if you make an adjustment to the length in the back, to make the corresponding change for the front.)

Armhole Shaping

On the next row, continuing in pattern established, bind off 2 sts at the beginning of the next 2 rows, then decrease 1 st at each end every other row 3 times. Work even until armhole measures 9 (9½, 10, 10½)".

Bind off 4 (5, 5, 6) sts at beginning of next 4 rows. Place 14 (14, 18, 18) sts on holder for neck.

Front

Work as for back until armhole measures 6 (6½, 7, 7½)". Work across 11 (13, 13, 15) sts, slip next 8 (8, 12, 12) sts on holder.
Joining a second ball of yarn, work the remaining 11 (13, 13, 15) sts. Continue working both sides of the front, decreasing 1 st at each neck

MATERIALS:

* Colinette Hand-Dyed *Point Five* (wool, 55 yds/100 gm hanks)— 8 (10, 12, 13) hanks

* Small amount of smooth-textured sport weight yarn for sewing seams

* Size 17 straight needles, or size to obtain gauge

* 2 stitch holders

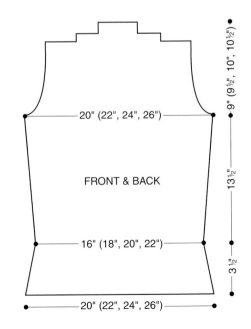

9" (9½", 10", 10½")

20" (22", 24", 26")

FRONT & BACK

13½"

16" (18", 20", 22")

3½"

20" (22", 24", 26")

edge every row 2 times, then every other row once. Work even until front is the same length as for back. Bind off as for shoulders on back.

Sleeves

Cast on 16 (16, 18, 20) sts. Increase 1 st at each end every 1½", 9 times, then work even until piece measures 17". Bind off 2 sts at beginning of next 2 rows. Decrease 1 st at each end every other row until sleeve cap measures 6 (6½, 7, 7½)". Decrease 2 sts at beginning of next 2 rows, then bind off remaining stitches.

🛑 In the finishing steps that follow, we repeatedly say, "bind off loosely," and there's a good reason for that. If you bind off tightly, the sweater will be difficult to get over your head and feel uncomfortable when you wear it. And when we say "loose," we mean real loose, so your stitches look oversized. (You will not even notice these loose stitches once you start wearing or block your sweater.) If you knit tightly, try binding off using a larger size needle.

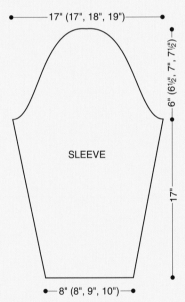

Photo: Christina L. Holmes

Finishing:

▽ Because of the texture of this yarn, we recommend sewing the seams with a smooth textured sport or worsted weight yarn, in a color that will blend in with the sweater yarn. Sew the left shoulder seam.

Collar

With RS facing, pick up neck sts on the holder, pick up sts along left neckline, sts from front neck holder and sts along front right neckline, approximately 44 (46, 52, 60) sts.

For those who prefer the jewel-neck collar, bind off the sts that you have picked up along the neck loosely and work one row of reverse single crochet (crab stitch) around it.

For the roll collar as pictured, work 6 rows of St st knit side out so it will roll and the purl side will show. Bind off loosely.

Sew right shoulder seam and collar. Sew side seams and sleeve seams, then set in sleeves. Work 1 row of reverse single crochet around the bottom of the bodice and sleeves.

Steam lightly if desired.

Chenille Scarf & Hat

Designed by Mary Colucci

Solid and printed yarns in coordinating colors give this scarf and hat set its subtle tweed look. Narrow shaping makes this scarf especially comfortable for wrapping, and it's light.

Scarf Size:

Scarf is approximately 6" wide and 54" long

Gauge:

With size 11 needle in Stockinette stitch, 5 sts = 3"
To ensure the proper size, take time to check your gauge.

Instructions:

The scarf is worked in Stockinette stitch, alternating colors every two rows. You do not have to cut the yarn when you change to the other color; simply drop one color yarn and pick up the second color. As you switch back and forth between colors, remember not to pull the yarn at the edges or the edges will pucker.
With color A cast on 10 sts.
Row 1: Knit
Row 2: Purl
Row 3: Pick up Color B, knit.
Row 4: Purl.
Repeat Rows 1 through 4 until the scarf measures 54" or the scarf length you desire, ending with two rows of Color A. Bind off and work in the yarn ends.

Hat Size:

This snug-fitting hat will fit head sizes 19-21". To increase the size, add two stitches per inch.

Instructions:

With size 15 needles and working with one strand of Color A and one strand Color B held together, cast on 25 stitches.
Rows 1-10: Working with Color A and Color B held together, k every stitch. Piece should measure approximately 3" from beginning.

SCARF MATERIALS:

❖ Lion Brand's Chenille *"Thick & Quick®"* (acrylic/rayon, 100 yd skein)
Wine (#189), Color A—1 skein
Ruby Print (#213), Color B—1 skein

❖ Size 11 needles, or size to obtain gauge

❖ Yarn needle to work in ends

HAT MATERIALS:

❖ Lion Brand's Chenille *"Thick & Quick®"* (acrylic/rayon, 100 yd skein)
Wine (#189), Color A—1 skein
Ruby Print (#213), Color B—1 skein

❖ Size 11 needles

❖ Size 15 needles

❖ Yarn needle to work in ends

*NOTE: One skein of each color will be sufficient to complete a hat and scarf of the approximate size noted in the scarf and hat pattern. Purchase additional yarn to ensure that you have enough yarn in the same dye lot if you plan to make significantly larger sizes.

Beginning with Row 11, switch to size 11 needles and begin St st pattern. (To switch needle size, simply hold one of the size 11 needles in your right hand and work the stitches off of the size 15 needle, following the pattern and continue knitting with the size 11 needles. Beginning with Row 11, you also will work with a single strand of yarn, rather than holding two strands together.

Row 11: With one strand of Color A, knit.

Row 12: Purl. (See note under Chenille Scarf pattern about alternating colors.)

Row 13: Pick up Color B, knit.

Row 14: Purl.

Repeat Rows 11 through 14 until the Stockinette piece measures approximately 6". Bind off leaving a long end of yarn to use for finishing.

Finishing:

You have knitted a rectangle. To finish the hat, sew the side seam with

Photo: Christina L. Holmes

the right side of the fabric facing the inside. The garter stitch panel frames your face. To complete the hat you have to join the stockinette end at the top. Thread a yarn needle with an 18" length of yarn (or the yarn end from the bind-off row) and carefully pick up the edges of stitches around the top of the hat. Gently gather the edges together, closing the top. To cover any open spaces, simply criss-cross the yarn several times, and secure by weaving in the ends. Cut the thread.

NOTE: Because *Thick & Quick* is a very furry yarn, using a non-textured sport or worsted weight yarn in a matching color might be easier for finishing. If you use *Thick & Quick* for finishing, remember to pull the yarn gently.

Loop-Trim Scarf

Designed by Christina L. Holmes

Tired of tassels? Frustrated with fringe? Here's a fast and easy—but different look, knitted with two strands and using a backstitch for the loop embellishment. An easy jaunt in cruise control at the speed limit!

Size:

Scarf measures 9½" x 48"

Gauge:

2 stitches = 1"
To ensure proper size, take time to check your gauge.

Instructions:

Holding two strands of MC, cast on 19 stitches. Work in St st, ▽ To form a selvedge to prevent rolling, knit the first 2 sts of each purl row. Work until scarf measures 48", then bind off and weave in any loose ends.

Finishing:

Loop Trim

Cut eight, 24' lengths of B; four, 24' lengths of A; and four, 24' lengths of C.

MATERIALS:
- ❖ Lion Brand *Jiffy*®, (acrylic, 3 oz/ 115 yd ball)

   Denver (#307) Main Color (MC)— 3 balls
   Violet (#191), Color A—1 ball
   Teal (#178), Color B—1 ball
   Navy (#110), Color C—1 ball

- ❖ Size 15 straight needles, or size to obtain gauge

- ❖ Yarn or tapestry needle with eye large enough to hold 4 strands of yarn

NOTE: Yes, we threaded our needles with all 24' of yarn. When we say *Knitting in the Fast Lane*, we mean it! We didn't want to weave in lots of ends. However, working with such a long "strand" can be challenging and unless you pull carefully, very wearing on the yarn, so it's best to cut it into more manageable lengths.

Thread four strands of A into yarn needle. Working in the last row lengthwise, secure yarn in first stitch, then work in backstitch the length of the scarf. Work each stitch over one stitch on the right side, leaving two stitches space between each loop. 🛑 To form loops, loop all four strands of yarn over forefinger when you bring the needle up on the right side of the scarf. Secure with knot at end of the scarf.

Follow this same pattern to make three more rows of loop trim, in B, C, then B again, leaving one stitch between rows.

Photo: Christina L. Holmes

The Warmest Scarf Ever!

Designed by Christina L. Holmes

Sometimes you prefer a scarf, sometimes a shawl; why not both? This hybrid measures 12" wide (not including the 5" fringe along the length) and 6' long, so it can double as a scarf or a shawl, depending on your mood, and it's warm as toast. You'll be breaking the speed limit on those size 35 needles with this lofty, lush yarn!

Size:

12" x 72" (not including fringe)

Gauge:

In Stockinette stitch with size 35 needle, 2½ stitches and 4 rows = 2"
To ensure the proper size, take time to check your gauge.

Instructions:

🔶 You will knit the first two stitches of every purl row to form a selvedge edge to prevent rolling.
Cast on 16 stitches in A. K 8 rows (garter stitch) for border. Join MC and work in St st until piece measures approximately 68½". 🛑 Be sure to knit the first two stitches of every purl row for a selvedge edge to prevent rolling. Remember to move the yarn to the front of your knitting for your purl stitches, then to the back of the knitting for the last two knit stitches in the row.
Join A and work for 8 rows in garter stitch for border. Bind off. Weave in yarn ends throughout.

MATERIALS:

❖ Horstia's *Marokko* from Muench Yarns (wool, 200 gm/80 meter hank)
Off White (#117) Main Color (MC)—3 hanks
Charcoal (#103), Color A—1 hank

❖ Size 35/19mm needles, or size to obtain gauge

❖ Large crochet hook for fringe (size J, for example, optional)

Fringe:

Hold one strand of MC and one strand of A together. Cut 53, 12" lengths. Fold each set in half, pull folded end through the last knit stitch, pull the end through that loop, and tighten. Attach at every other stitch along the length. (You can use a large crochet hook or even your fingers to pull the doubled yarn through each stitch, since the yarn is so thick.)

Photo: Christina L. Holmes

Cabled & Cozy Afghan

Designed by Lion Brand Yarn Co.

Love those cables! Three plump cable panels knitted with three strands held together on size 19 needles will give you the warmest blanket ever—and a decorating showpiece as well.

Size:

Approximately 41" by 56" without border
NOTE: Entire afghan is worked holding three strands of yarn held together.

Because of the thickness of the yarns, the afghan is constructed in panels of 40 stitches. Make three. Each panel measures approximately 14" wide.

Gauge:

Holding 3 strands of yarn on size 19 needles in Stockinette stitch, 3 sts = 2"
To ensure proper size, take time to check your gauge.

Pattern Stitch:

Rows 1, 3, 5, 7, 9 & 11: P2, k2, p32, k2, p2.
Rows 2, 4, 8, 10, & 12: K2, p2, k32, p2, k2.
Row 6 (cable row): K2, p2, sl 8 sts to cable needle and hold in back, k 8 sts; k the 8 from cable needle; slip next 8 sts and hold in front; k 8; k 8 from cable needle, p2, k2.

Afghan Panel (make three):

With size 19 needles and holding 3 strands of yarn together, cast on 40 sts. Work in pattern for 11 repeats, ending with Row 12. Panel measures approximately 56". Bind off.

Finishing:

Using 2 strands of yarn held together, sew the panels together, taking 1 stitch from each side. Tack the edges of each cable on the cast on and bind off rows so that they do not fan out and are in proportion to the rest of the cables.

MATERIALS:

❖ Lion Brand's *Jiffy*™ (acrylic, 3 oz/ 115 yd ball)

  Fisherman (#099)—33 balls

❖ Size 17 knitting needles

❖ Size 19 knitting needles, or size to obtain gauge

❖ Cable needle ▽ (Because you will be working with three strands of yarn, you may not be able to find a large enough cable needle to hold 8 stitches. Substitute a double pointed needle.)

❖ Yarn or tapestry needle for finishing

Borders:

Top and Bottom

Using size 17 needles and 3 strands of yarn, cast on 7 sts. Work in Seed St as follows:
Row 1: K1, *p1, k1; rep from *. Repeat this row for 42".

Using 2 strands of yarn held together, sew the borders to the top and bottom edges, taking a full st from each piece.

Side Borders

Cast on and work as for top and bottom borders for 63". Position side borders along afghan and top and bottom borders and sew as above.

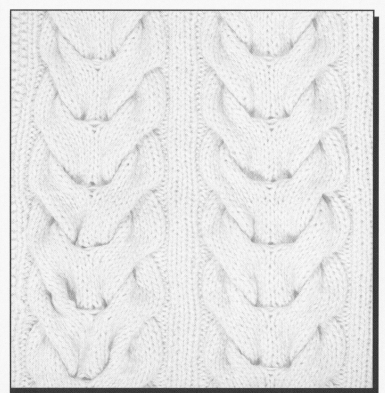

Photo: Christina L. Holmes

Button-Down Bag

Designed by Arnetta Kenney

This shoulder bag has no gussets, just two sides in an interesting stitch, worked with three strands held together on size 13 needles. Throw it over your shoulder for a sporty, fashion look with the luxury feel of alpaca.

Size:

Approximately 12" by 15" flat (when flap is folded over approximate size 12" by 9")

Gauge:

With size 13 needle in garter stitch and 3 strands of yarn, 11 sts = 4".
To ensure proper sizing, take time to check gauge.

MATERIALS:

❖ Lion Brand's *AL*PA*KA*
  (alpaca/wool/acrylic, 50 gm/107 yd ball)
  Camel (#124)—9 skeins

❖ Size 13 straight knitting needles, or needle size to obtain gauge

❖ 1 Large button for closure

❖ Yarn or tapestry needle for finishing

Loop Pattern:

STOP Slip all sts purlwise.
Row 1: (right side): Knit.
Row 2: * K1, slip 1; repeat from * to last 2 sts, k2.
Row 3: Knit.
Row 4: K2, * slip 1, k1; repeat from * to end.
Repeat these 4 rows.

Instructions:

NOTE: Bag is knitted with three strands of yarn together.

Side 1

Using 3 strands of yarn held together, cast on 34 sts.

Rows 1–6: Work 6 rows in Garter St.

Rows 7–13: Beginning with Row 1 of loop pattern (WS), work from row 1 to row 4 of loop pattern once. Then work from row 1 to row 3 of pattern once. (WS should be facing).

Repeat rows 1-13 until piece measures 14", ending with all or part of Rows 1-6 in garter st.

Flap

Row 1: Purl.

Row 2: Knit.

Row 3: Purl.

Row 4: Purl.

Rows 5–7: K 1 row, p1 row, ending with WS facing.

Rows 8–11: Work from row 1 to row 4 of loop pattern once.

Rows 12–13: Work garter st pattern for two rows. Bind off.

Side 2

Work the same as Side 1, until piece measures 14", ending with right side facing, before beginning the flap.

Strap

Using size 13 needles and three strands held together, cast on 6 sts. Work in garter stitch until strap measures 25" (or desired length).  Avoid making the strap too long as it will stretch with use.

Finishing:

Using a large tapestry needle, with two strands of yarn and right sides facing, sew the bag together at bottom and side edges using an overcast stitch.

To attach the strap, fold down the top edge of the bag approximately 5½". Fasten strap ends along the fold edge on both sides with an overcast stitch.

For the loop closure, cut two lengths of yarn approximately 4" long, twist loosely and attach to the top piece of the back flap just above the garter stitch border. Sew a large button onto front side of the bag, below the button loop.

Doggie Bed Pillow

Designed by Kathleen Sams for Coats & Clark

Woof, woof. Sweaters aren't the only things to knit for your dog. Here's another idea, a bed pillow shaped like a bone. Your dog will love the cushy thickness of the yarn and you'll love the fact that it's fast to knit and easy care.

Size:

21" x 27"

Gauge:

In Stockinette stitch and size 17 needles, 2 sts = 1".
To ensure proper sizing, take time to check your gauge.

Instructions:

Back & Front

With 3 strands of yarn held together as one, cast on 48 sts.
Row 1 (RS): Knit.
Row 2: Purl.
*Row 3: K 11; TURN. ◇CAUTION◇ To shape the dog bed pillow, you will work what are called "short rows," which like its name suggests you knit only part of a row, in this case 11 stitches. With 11 stitches on your right needle, simply turn your work so the 11 stitches are now in your left hand and the other stitches in your right. Now you are ready to purl the 11 stitches. In subsequent rows when it says to knit 12, 13 and 14 stitches, simply pick up an additional stitch and continue working. At Row 20 you will work the 14 stitches of the short row and continue knitting the remaining 34 stitches.

MATERIALS:

❖ Red Heart® *Super Saver®* (acrylic, 6 oz/348 yd skein)
Shaded Browns (#992)—3 skeins

❖ Size 17/12.75mm, or size to obtain gauge

❖ Filling (See note below.)

▽ Some dogs will love this bed pillow without any stuffing. If you want a really soft bed, consider using 2, 14" pillow forms for the center of the bone and 4, 8" round pillows for the ends. Another option is creating a casing from an old towel or pillowcase, filling it with a large bag of polyester fiberfill and stuffing the bed.

Row 4: P 11.	**Row 16:** P 13; turn.	**Row 28:** K 12.	**Row 40:** K 48 sts.
Row 5: K 12; turn.	**Row 17:** K 13.	**Row 29:** P 11; turn.	**Row 41:** P 14; turn.
Row 6: P 12.	**Row 18:** P 14; turn.	**Row 30:** K 11.	**Row 42:** K 14.
Row 7: K 13; turn.	**Row 19:** K 14.	**Row 31:** P 48 sts.	**Row 43:** P 13; turn.
Row 8: P 13.	**Row 20:** P 48 sts.	**Row 32:** K 14; turn.	**Row 44:** K 13.
Row 9: K 14; turn.	**Row 21.** K 48 sts.	**Row 33:** P 14.	**Row 45:** P 12; turn.
Row 10: P 14.	**Row 22:** P 48 sts.	**Row 34:** K 13; turn.	**Row 46:** K 12.
Row 11: K across 48 sts.	**Row 23:** P 14; turn.	**Row 35:** P 13.	**Row 47:** P 11; turn.
Row 12: P 11; turn.	**Row 24:** K 14.	**Row 36:** K 12; turn.	**Row 48:** K 11.
Row 13: K 11.	**Row 25:** P 13; turn.	**Row 37:** P 12.	**Row 49:** P 48 sts. **
Row 14: P 12; turn.	**Row 26:** K 13.	**Row 38:** K 11; turn.	
Row 15: K 12.	**Row 27:** P 12; turn.	**Row 39:** P 11.	

Photo: Christina L. Holmes

Bind off 14 sts, k across. Next Row: Bind off 14 sts, p across. Beginning with k row, work in St st to 14", end p row.

Cast on 14 sts. K across—34 sts. Cast on 14 sts. P across—48 sts. Repeat from * to **. Bind off.

Finishing:

With right sides together, sew seams. Leave opening if you plan to stuff.

Chapter 4

Around Town

Hooded Seed–Stitch Jacket

Designed by Ann E. Smith for Coats & Clark

Casual and comfy, this hooded jacket is worked in seed stitch using three strands of yarn on size 15 needles for speed. The simple stitch creates a pattern of texture, and contrast edging is worked in crochet.

Sizes:

Directions are for women's sizes Small (Medium, Large, X-Large)
Finished bust size (buttoned), 40 (42, 44, 46)"
Finished Length: 19½ (20½, 21½, 22½)"

Gauge:

With size 15 needles in seed stitch and 3 strands of yarn held
together, 5 sts and 7 rows = 2"
To ensure the proper fit, take time to check your gauge.

Pattern Stitch:

NOTE: Use 3 strands of yarn held together throughout this project.
Seed Stitch (also known as Moss Stitch)
Row 1: * K1, p1 repeat from * across row
Row 2: * P1, k1 repeat from * across row
Repeat these two rows for pattern.

Instructions:

Back
With MC and three strands of yarn, cast on 50 (52, 55, 57) sts.
Work seed st to 17½ (18½, 19½, 20½)" from beginning.
Bind off in seed st.

MATERIALS:

❖ Red Heart® *Soft* (Bounce-Back®
   acrylic, 5 oz/328 yd skein)
   New Aran (#7313), Main Color
   (MC)—7 (9, 9, 10) skeins
   Dk. Yellow Green (#7675)
   Contrasting Color (CC)—3 skeins

❖ Size 15/10mm knitting needles, or
   size to obtain gauge

❖ Size K/10½ aluminum crochet
   hook

❖ Yarn or tapestry needle for finishing

❖ 5, 1⅛" buttons

❖ 2 stitch markers

Front
(Make two): With MC and three strands of
yarn cast on 22 (24, 25, 26) sts. Work seed st
for 1".
For Pocket Opening: At the beginning of the
next row, bind off 3 sts in seed st. Work even
for 5". Cast on 3 sts above pocket opening.
Continue as established to 15½ (16½, 17½,
18½)" from beginning.

Photo: Christina L. Holmes

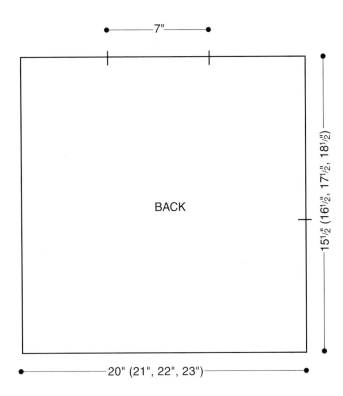

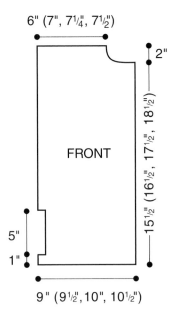

Neck Shaping

At the beginning of the next row (on opposite edge from pocket opening), bind off 5 sts in seed st. Decrease 1 st at neck every other row twice. Work even on remaining 15 (17, 18, 19) sts to same length as back. Bind off in seed st.

Sleeve (Make two)

With MC and three strands of yarn, cast on 25 (26, 27, 29) sts. Work in seed st, increase 1 st each edge every 4th row 10 (11, 12, 12) times; include these new sts into pattern 45 (48, 51, 53) sts. When piece measures 14 (14½, 14¾, 15)" from beginning, bind off in seed st.

Pocket (Make two)

With MC, cast on 12 sts. Work seed st for 5". Bind off in seed st.

Hood

With MC, cast on 54 sts. Work seed st for 9". At the beginning of the next 2 rows, bind off 18 sts in seed st.

For Back

Work even on center 18 sts until piece measures 16" from beginning. Bind off in seed st. Using one strand of yarn, sew bound-off sts of each side to sides of hood back.

Finishing:

Join shoulder seams. From each side of the shoulder seams, measure down 9½ (10, 10½, 11)" and place markers. Set in sleeves between markers.

With WS facing, place pocket onto front so that it covers the indention at side opening. Leaving an opening at seam, sew pockets to inside of fronts. With the RS facing, using crochet hook, join MC with a slip st to edge of pocket opening on front only.

Row 1: Ch 1, sc evenly across; DO NOT TURN.
Row 2: Ch 1, working from left to right, sc in each sc across for reverse sc. Fasten off. Join sides of pocket edging to sides of pocket opening. Join sleeve and side seams, sewing pockets (not the crochet border) into seam.

Body Edging

With the RS facing using 3 strands of CC and crochet hook, join with a slip st in corner of left front neck edge. Ch 1, work 28 (30, 32, 34) sc evenly spaced to corner, 3 sc in corner, sc evenly along lower edge.

▽ (For an attractive edge, do not sc crochet into every stitch across the bottom. Skip approximately every 6th st) 78 (84, 90, 96) sts, 3 sc in corner, 28 (30, 32, 34) sc along right front; turn.

Row 2: Ch 3, dc in each sc around working 3 dc in each corner; turn.
Row 3: Ch 1, sc in each dc around; DO NOT TURN.
Row 4: Ch 1, working from left to right, sc in each sc around for reverse sc; fasten off.

Cuff

With the WS facing and crochet hook, join CC with slip st in lower sleeve seam. Ch 1, work 25 (26, 27, 29) dc around; join with slip st in 3rd ch of beginning ch 3.
Round 2: Ch 3, dc in each st around; join with slip st in 3rd ch of beginning ch 3. Repeat Round 2 for 4 times more. Ch 1, work reverse sc around and fasten off.

Hood

RSs together, pin hood onto MC neck edge at each side of Body Edging and ease to fit. With crochet hook and MC, slip st in place. With RS of hood facing, join CC with slip st in edge.

Row 1: Ch 1, work about 55 sc evenly spaced across; DO NOT TURN.
Row 2: Ch 1, working from left to right, sc in each sc for reverse sc; fasten off.

Buttons

Sew buttons 1" from neck and lower edges then space remaining 3 buttons at even intervals between the first 2. Push buttons through the dc row. Turn back cuffs.

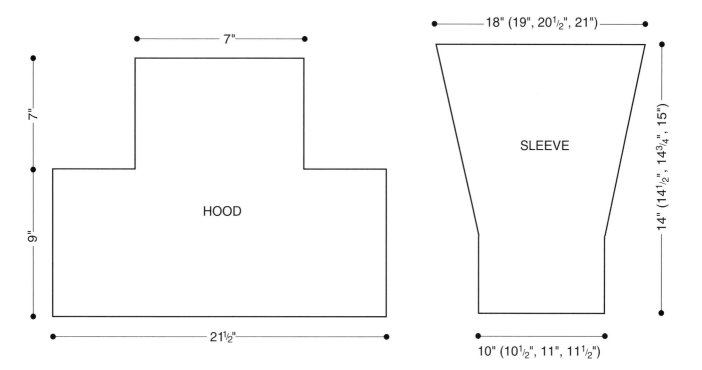

Basketweave Jacket

Designed by Ann E. Smith for Coats & Clark

Toss on this raglan-sleeved cardigan for running errands and you'll always feel "dressed." The textured yarn and stitch jazz up this practical look, rounded out by handy pockets. Test drive the Body Pattern before you begin. Once you master the combination of knit and purl stitches, you'll understand why basketweave is a favorite knitters' route.

Sizes:

Instructions are for women's sizes Small (Medium, Large, and X-large)
Finished Bust (Buttoned): 41½ (45½, 49, 52½)"
Finished Length: 26 (26½, 27, 28)"

Gauge:

In Body Pattern with size 11 needles, 11 sts and 15 rows = 5"

MATERIALS:

❖ Red Heart® *Light & Lofty*™ (acrylic, 6 oz/148 yd skein)
   Cafe Au Lait (# 9334)—5(6, 6, 7) skeins

❖ Size 10 knitting needles

❖ Size 11 knitting needles, or size needed to obtain gauge

❖ Yarn needle

❖ 3 stitch holders

❖ Five, 1⅛ inch diameter buttons

The following Body Pattern creates a basketweave pattern (alternating blocks of knit and purl stitches). The designer added rows of rib stitch to separate and define the basketweave pattern. Please note that throughout the instructions, the phrase: "keep continuity of pattern, adjusting stitches accordingly" is mentioned. This means that in certain sizing changes and when increasing or decreasing stitches be careful to maintain the established pattern (Body Pattern) on the main part of the sweater and adjust the pattern along the side edges.

Photo: Christina L. Holmes

Body Pattern (multiple of 10 + 5):

Row 1 (RS): *(K1, p1) 2 times, k1, p5; repeat from * across to last 5 sts (k1, p1) 2 times, k1.

Row 2: *(P1, k1) 2 times, p6; repeat from * across to last 5, (p1, k1) 2 times, p1.

Row 3: *(K1, p1) 2 times, k6; repeat from * across to last 5, (k1, p1) 2 times, k1.

Row 4: *(P1, k1) 2 times, p1, k5; repeat from * across to last 5 sts, (p1, k1) 2 times, p1.

Row 5: Repeat Row 3.

Row 6: Repeat Row 2.

Row 7: Repeat Row 1.

Row 8: Repeat Row 2.

Row 9: Repeat Row 3.

Row 10: Repeat Row 4.

Row 11: Repeat Row 3.

Row 12: *K5, (p1, k1) 2 times, p1; repeat from * across.

Row 13: *K6, (p1, k1) 2 times; repeat from * across to last 5 sts, k5.

Row 14: *P6, *(k1, p1) 2 times; repeat from * across to last 5 sts, p5.

Row 15: *P5, (k1, p1) 2 times, k1; repeat from * across.

Row 16: Repeat Row 14.

Row 17: Repeat Row 13.

Row 18: Repeat Row 12.

Row 19: Repeat Row 13.

Row 20: Repeat Row 14.

Row 21: Repeat Row 15.

Row 22: Repeat Row 14.

Repeat Rows 1-22 for Body Pattern.

Instructions:

Jacket Back

With size 10 needles cast on 41 (45, 49, 53) sts. Work in ribbing as follows:

Row 1 (RS): K1, * p1, k1; repeat from * across.

Row 2: P1, *k1, p1; repeat from * across. Repeat Rows 1 and 2 for 3", increase 4 (5, 6, 7) sts evenly on last row, end Row 2 – 45 (50, 55, 60) sts. Change to size 11 needles and work in Body Pattern, adjusting stitches accordingly.

Keeping continuity of pattern, adjusting stitches accordingly, work until 16¼ (16¼, 16½, 17)" from beginning, end WS row.

Shape Raglans

Bind off 3 (3, 4, 4) sts at beginning of next 2 rows. K1, slip 1, k1, psso, work in pattern to last 3 sts, k2tog, k1. Work 1 row even. Decrease 1 st each edge as before every other row until there are 11 (14, 15, 18) sts. Work even to 26 (26½, 27, 28)" from beginning, end WS row. Place sts on a holder.

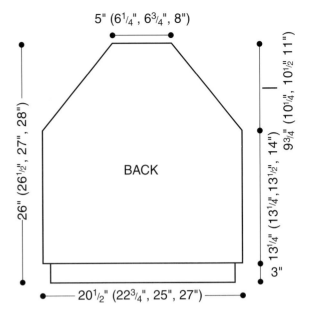

5" (6¼", 6¾", 8")

BACK

26" (26½", 27", 28")

13¼" (13¼, 13½, 14")

9¾" (10¼, 10½ 11")

3"

20½" (22¾", 25", 27")

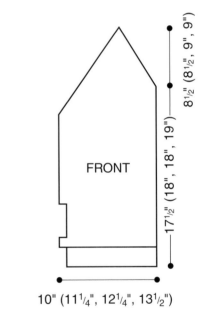

8½" (8½", 9", 9")

FRONT

17½" (18", 18", 19")

10" (11¼", 12¼", 13½")

Left Front

With size 10 needles, cast on 19 (21, 23, 25) sts. Work in ribbing same as for Back for 3", increase 3 (4, 4, 5) sts evenly spaced on last row, end Row 2—22 (25, 27, 30) sts. Change to size 11 needles and work in Body Pattern, adjusting stitches accordingly. AT THE SAME TIME when piece measures 6" from beginning, bind off 3 sts at beginning of next row for Pocket Opening. Work even on remaining 19 (22, 24, 27) sts for 15 rows. Keeping continuity of pattern, cast on 3 sts at end of next row – 22 (25, 27, 30) sts. Continue in pattern to 16¼ (16¼, 16½, 17)", end WS row.

Shape Raglan as for back. AT THE SAME TIME when 17½ (18, 18, 19)" from beginning, begin V-neck shaping.

V-Neck Shaping

Decrease 1 st at neck edge on next row, then every right side row 1 (1, 1, 2) times, then every 6th row 2 (3, 3, 3) times. Work same as for back. Place sts on a holder.

Right Front

Work same as left front, reversing shaping.

Sleeves

With size 10 needles, cast on 21 (21, 23, 23) sts. Work in ribbing same as for back for 3" increase 4 (4, 7, 7) sts evenly spaced on last row, end Row 2—25 (25, 30, 30) sts. ⬦CAUTION Change to size 11 needles and work in pattern as for back, shaping sides by increasing 1 st each end of next row, then every 6th row until there are 41 (43, 48, 50) sts. Work even in established pattern until 16½ (16½, 17¼, 18)" from beginning, end WS row.

Shape Raglans

Work same as for back until there are 7 sts. Continue in pattern until 26¼ (27, 28, 29)" from beginning, end WS row. Place sts on a holder.

Pocket Linings (Make 2)

With size 10 needles, cast on 11 sts. Beginning with Purl row, work 17 rows in St st. Bind off loosely.

Finishing:

Pocket Trim

With RS facing and size 10 needles, pick up and k 11 sts evenly spaced along opening. Work 3 rows ribbing as for back. Bind off loosely in ribbing. Join sides of pocket to top and bottom of opening. Join pocket lining to back opening so RS is next to WS of front. Sew pocket in place.

Sew raglan seams. Join side and arm seams, leaving pocket open.

Right Front Band and Buttonholes

With right side facing and size 10 needles, pick up and k 43 (45, 45, 47) sts evenly spaced up edge to V-neck. Work 2 rows ribbing same as for Back.
Row 3: Rib 2 (2, 2, 4) sts, yo, k2tog; *(p1, k1) 3 times, p1, yo, p2tog, (k1, p1) 3 times, k1, yo, k2tog; repeat from * again, rib to end. Work 3 more rows in ribbing. Bind off loosely in ribbing.

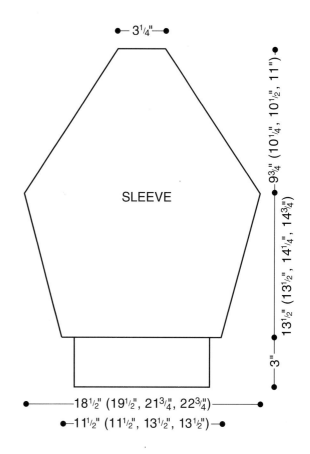

SLEEVE

3¼"

9¾" (10¼, 10½, 11")

13½" (13½, 14¼, 14¾)

3"

18½" (19½, 21¾, 22¾")

11½" (11½, 13½, 13½")

Left Front Band

With RS facing and size 10 needles, begin at V-neck, pick up and k 43 (45, 45, 47) sts evenly spaced down edge. Work in ribbing as for back for 6 rows. Bind off loosely in ribbing. Sew buttons opposite buttonholes.

Collar

With RS facing and size 10 needles, pick up and k 6 sts evenly along top of right front band, stitches from the holders and 6 sts along top of left band. Work 7 rows in ribbing as for back. At beginning of next 8 rows, bind off 7 sts loosely in ribbing. Bind off remaining sts.

Weekend Wrap-Up

Designed by Kathleen Sams for Coats & Clark

Wrap up for any trip around town with this sporty ruana. There are "no detours" with this pattern, just a "fork" in the road where you work two sides of the center panel (there are three panels), creating the front opening. This lightweight yarn is comfortable to wear in addition to being fast to knit, especially on size 17s.

Size:

Measures 43" across back, 24" at center and 32" at inner front edge

Gauge:

In Stockinette stitch and size 17 needles, 12 rows and 8 sts = 4". To ensure proper fit, take time to check your gauge.

Instructions:

Back

With A, cast on 46 sts. Work in St st (k1 row, p1 row) for 10 rows. Continuing in St st, work in stripe pattern as follows:

1 Row B	1 Row A	4 Rows A
2 Rows C	2 Rows B	1 Row B
1 Row B	1 Row A	2 Rows C
4 Rows A	2 Rows C	1 Row B
2 Rows C		

Change to A and continue in St st for 25". Next Row: K across 23 sts. Put remaining 23 sts on a holder. Continue in St st working stripe pattern in reverse, then change to A and work an additional 11 rows, end purl row. Bind off. With RS facing, join yarn to remaining 23 sts, k to end. Complete to correspond to first side. Bind off.

Side Panels (Make 2)

With B cast on 23 sts. **Row 1 (RS):** Knit. **Row 2:** P to last 3 sts, k3. Repeat Rows 1 and 2 to 48". Bind off.

Finishing:

Keeping garter stitch of side panels on outer edge, sew side panels to the sides of the back panel.

MATERIALS:

❖ Red Heart® *Light & Lofty*™ (acrylic, 6 oz/148 yd skein)
  Navy Grape (#9387), Color A— 2 skeins
  Wine (#9376), Color B—2 skeins
  Creamsicle (#9322), Color C— 1 skein

❖ Size 17/12.75mm circular knitting needles, or size to obtain gauge

❖ Stitch holder

❖ Yarn or tapestry needle for finishing

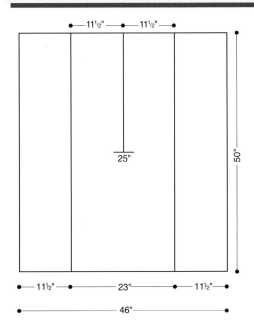

Photo: Christina L. Holmes

Chapter 5
Shore Things

Starry Crop Top

Designed by Ann E. Smith for Coats & Clark

This cropped top is a great summer look over a bikini top or tube top. Test-drive the Star Cluster stitch in your gauge swatch and you'll have a quick trip to the beach!

Sizes:

Directions are for women's sizes Extra Small (Small, Medium, Large, X-Large)
Finished Bust: 31 (35½, 39, 40, 42)"
Length: 13½ (14, 14½, 15½, 16½)"

Gauge:

Using two strands of yarn and size 13 needles, 18 sts = 5", 16 rows = 4"
To ensure the proper fit, take time to check your gauge.

Pattern Stitch:

Star Cluster (a multiple of 4 sts + 2 sts; a repeat of 4 rows)
Row 1: (RS) K1 * k2tog, (yo) twice, k2tog through the back loop of the sts (this twists the stitches); repeat from * across, ending k1.
Row 2: P2; * p1 (the first yo), p1 in the back loop of the stitch (the second yo), cluster the next 2 sts as follows (sl 2, purlwise, with yarn in back, bring yarn to front between needles, slip the same 2 sts back to left-hand needle, pass yarn to back between needles, slip the same 2 sts with the yarn in back again); repeat from * across ending p1, p1 into the back loop of the st, p2.
Row 3: K3; * k2tog, (yo) twice, k2tog in back loop of sts; repeat from * across, ending k3.
Row 4: P2; * cluster 2, p1, p1 in back loop of the st; repeat from * across, ending cluster 2, p2.

MATERIALS:

❖ Aunt Lydia's® *Denim* (cotton/acrylic, 400 yd ball)
   Red (#1003)—2 balls for all sizes

❖ Size 9/5.5mm knitting needles

❖ Size 13/9mm knitting needles, or size needed to obtain gauge

❖ Yarn or tapestry needle for finishing

❖ Size 9/I aluminum crochet hook

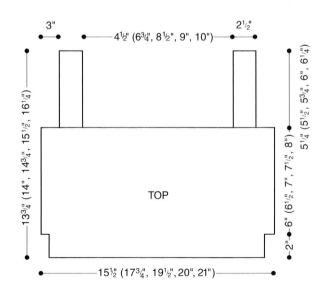

Instructions:

Back

Beginning at the lower edge with smaller needles and two strands of yarn held together, cast on 53 (61, 65, 69, 73) sts.

Row 1: (WS) P1, (k1, p1) across.

Row 2: K1, (p1, k1) across.

Repeat rows 1–2 to 2" from beginning, ending with a WS row and increase 1 st, 54 (62, 68, 70, 74) sts.

⬦ Change to size 13 needles and begin Star Cluster pattern, continue even to 8 (8½, 9, 9½, 10)" from beginning, ending with a RS row. Next row, p across, working p1 in first yo and p1 in back loop of st in second yo. Bind off knitwise.

Front

Work as for back.

Straps (Make two)

Using two strands of yarn and size 9 needles, cast on 9 (9, 9, 11, 11) sts. Work ribbing as for back to 10½ (11, 11½, 12, 12½)" from beginning, ending with a WS row. Bind off in ribbing.

Finishing:

Join side seams.

Bodice Edging

With RS facing and crochet hook, join two strands of yarn near one top underarm seam with a slip st. Ch 1, sc evenly around, ending with slip st in first sc; turn. Ch 1, slip st in each sc around and fasten off.

Photo: Christina L. Holmes

Straps

With WS facing, place markers 3" from each side of first side seam. Pin strap to bodice so that there is a 6" space between strap sides at the underarm. Sew strap securely to the slipped stitch row of edging. Repeat for second strap.

Bodice Tie

Using two strands of yarn and crochet hook, ch 175 (201, 225, 252, 275). Slip st in 2nd ch from hook and in each ch across. Fasten off. Insert the tie along the top edge of the bodice in last row 3 of Star Clusters, begin at the center front, weaving the tie around the top edge. Tie into a bow. Tie ends into over-hand knots. Hide ends.

Fringe Benefits Top & Miniskirt

Designed by Kathleen Sams for Coats & Clark

Head to the beach in this top and miniskirt. It's the perfect bathing suit cover-up, and you'll love how fast knitting with two strands of yarn can be. We used multi-colored pearl-finish pony beads on the fringe; you might opt for wooden beads or none.

Sizes:

Directions are for women's sizes Small (Medium, Large)
Finished chest size: 34-36 (38-40, 42-44)"
Finished skirt length: 14 (15, 16)"
Finished Hip Size: 34-36 (38-40, 42-44)"

Gauge:

In Stockinette stitch and larger needle,
     12 sts and 16 rows = 4"
To ensure proper fit, take time to check your gauge.

NOTE: Work with 2 strands held together as one throughout.

Instructions:

Skirt Back

With larger needles and two strands of yarn, cast on 48 (54, 60) sts. **Row 1 (RS):** Knit. **Row 2:** P 2, k 2, * p4, k2; repeat from * across to last 2, p2. **Rows 3-4:** Repeat last 2 rows once more. **Rows 5, 7:** Knit. **Row 6, 8:** Purl. **Row 9:** Knit. **Row 10:** P5, * k2, p5; repeat from * across. **Rows 11-12:** Repeat Rows 9 and 10. **Rows 13-16:** Repeat Rows 5-8. **Rows 17-24:** Repeat Rows 1-8.
Continue working in St st (k1 row, p1 row) to 10 (11, 12)" from beginning or desired length.

Waistband

Change to size 11 needles. Work in Rib Pattern as follows: Row 1 (RS): * K 2, p 2; repeat from * across. Repeat last row until piece measures 14 (15, 16)", or desired length, working elastic thread through last 3 rows. Bind off in rib.

MATERIALS:

❖ Red Heart® *"Soft"* (*Bounce Back*® acrylic, 5 oz/328 yd skein) Medium Blue (#7821)—4 skeins

❖ Size 11/8mm circular needles

❖ Size 13/9mm circular needles, or size to obtain gauge

❖ Elastic thread

❖ 48 pony beads (optional)

❖ Yarn or tapestry needle for finishing

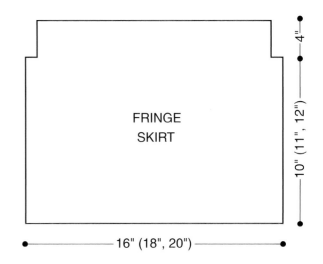

FRINGE
SKIRT

4"

10" (11", 12")

16" (18", 20")

Skirt Front

Work same as back.

Finishing:

With RS together, sew side seams. Weave in ends.

Top Back

With larger size needles and two strands of yarn, cast on 42 (48, 54) sts. K 4 rows. **Row 1 (RS):** Knit. **Row 2:** Purl. Repeat rows 1-2 to 6 (7, 8)", ending p row.

Shape Armhole

P 3, k across to last 3, purl 3. Next Row: P. Repeat last two rows until piece measures 13½ (15, 16½)" or desired length.

Shape Neck & Shoulders

Bind off 15, K across to last 3 sts, p 3. Next row, bind off 15. Put center 18 sts on a holder.

Top Front

Work same as back.

Finishing:

Roll Neck

With RS together, sew right shoulder seam. With RS facing, pick up and k 18 sts from front holder, 2 sts across seam, 18 sts from back holder. Purl next row, increase first stitch on each end—40 sts. Work in St st for 6 rows. Bind off. Sew remaining shoulder and neck seams. Sew side seams. Weave in ends.

Fringe

Cut 48, 9" lengths of yarn. Fold each strand of yarn in half, pull through bottom stitch of the hem as you would a fringe. Twist the doubled strand for the entire length, slip on one bead and knot at the end. (Make sure the knots are made at the very end so the beads hang even when worn.) Leave two stitches between each fringe.

Photo: Christina L. Holmes

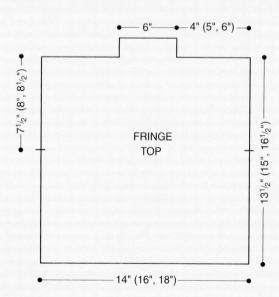

Chapter 6

Night Lights

Classic Cardigan

Designed by Elena Malo

Here's the classic cardigan jacket, sparkling with style. Holding three strands of different yarns (metallic ribbon, furry mohair and textured novelty), you'll work in Stockinette stitch on size 13 needles, and use two strands for the "fur" trim around the collar and cuffs. You'll be tempted to wear this over everything from jeans to velvet!

Sizes:
Women's sizes Small (Medium, Large, X-Large)
Finished garment at chest measures 40 (44, 48, 52)"

Gauge:
In Stockinette stitch with size 13 needles and one strand of A,B,C held together, 11 sts and 14 rows = 4"
To ensure proper fit, take time to check your gauge.

Instructions:

Back
Using one strand each of A, B and C, cast on 56 (60, 64, 68) sts. Work in garter st for 5 rows. Continue in St st until piece measures 14" from start.

Shape Armholes
Bind off 4 (4, 4, 5) sts at the beginning of next 2 rows, 2 sts at the beginning of next 2 rows, decrease 1 st each side, every other row 2 (3, 4, 4) times. 40 (42, 44, 48) sts. Work until armholes measure 8 (8½, 9, 9½)".

Shape Shoulders
Bind off 6 (7, 7, 8) sts at the beginning of next 4 (2, 4, 2) rows, 0 (6, 0, 8) at the beginning of the next 2 rows. Place remaining 16 sts on a stitch holder for back of neck.

Left Front
Cast on 32 (34, 36, 40) sts. Work 5 rows in garter st. Continue in St st, work in garter st over last 4 sts. Keeping to pattern as established, work until piece measures 14".

Shape Armhole
Bind off 4 (5, 5, 5) sts at the beginning of next row, 2 sts at the beginning of next row, decrease 1 st every RS row 3 (3, 4, 5) times. Continue on 23 (24, 25, 28) sts until armhole measures 6 (6½, 7, 7)" from beginning.

MATERIALS:

- Berroco *Optik* (cotton/acrylic/mohair/metallic/polyester, 87 yds, 50 gm hank)
  Matisse (#4902) Color A—9 (9, 10, 10) hanks
- Berroco *Metallica* (rayon/metallic, 85 yds, 25 gm hank)
  Gold (#1001) Color B—9 (9, 10, 10) hanks
- Berroco *Furz* (nylon/wool/acrylic, 90 yds, 50 gm hank)
  Wall Street Navy (#3806) Color C— 10 (10, 11, 11) balls

- 5, 1" navy coat buttons

- Size 13/9mm straight needles, or size needle to obtain gauge

- 3 stitch holders

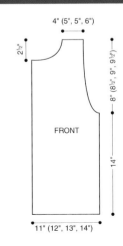

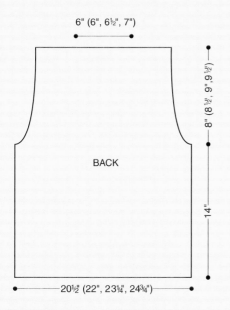

6" (6", 6½", 7")

8" (8½", 9", 9½")

14"

BACK

20½" (22", 23¼", 24¾")

Shape Neckline

Bind off 6 sts at the beginning of next WS row, then 2 sts once on the following WS row, decrease 1 st at neck edge every other row, 3 times.

Shape Shoulder

Bind off 6 (6, 7, 9) sts at the beginning of next RS row; bind off remaining 6 (7, 7, 8) sts. Place a marker for 5 buttonholes along front edge, evenly spaced between top of neckline and 1" from bottom edge.

Right Front

Work same as for left but reverse all shaping. Form 1 buttonhole to correspond to each marker as follows: k2tog, yo twice, slip 1, k 1, psso. Next row k1 from front, k1 from back in yo twice.

Sleeve

With 3 strands of C, cast on 32 (32, 34, 34) sts. Work in garter st for 11 rows. Change to 1 strand each of A , B and C, continue in St st, increasing 1 st each edge on first row, repeat increase every 6 (6, 4, 4) rows 7 (3, 0, 0) times, then every 4 rows, 0 (5, 8, 9) times, 48 (50, 52, 54) sts.

Shape Cap

Bind off 4 (4, 5, 5) sts at the beginning of next 2 rows, decrease 1 st each edge 14 (14, 14, 15) times, bind off remaining 12 (14, 14, 14) sts.

Finishing:

Seam shoulders. With RS facing you, and using 3 strands of C, pick up 44 sts from neckline edge, 14 sts along left front, 16 sts from the back neck, and 14 sts along right front. Work in garter st for 8 rows, bind off from WS. Seam sides, sleeve seams, sew in sleeves. Finish off all ends. Sew on buttons.

Photo: Christina L. Holmes

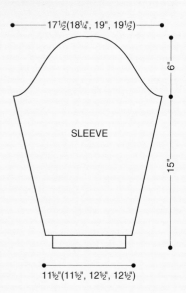

17½"(18¼", 19", 19½")

6"

SLEEVE

15"

11½"(11½", 12½", 12½")

Summer Evening Halter

Designed by Elena Malo

Take a modified halter top, add some sexy lacing across the back to adjust as much as you dare, and you've got an eye-catching evening look. Knit in one piece on size 11 needles, this design is worked with two strands of different yarns to combine sparkle and texture. (**NOTE:** although the schematic shows only one strap, there is one from each shoulder.)

Sizes:

Directions are for women's sizes Small (Medium, Large, X-Large) Finished garment at chest measures 36 (38, 40, 42)"

Gauge:

In Stockinette stitch (using 1 strand of A and 1 strand of B together) and size 11 needle, 14 sts and 22 rows = 4" To ensure the proper fit, take time to check your gauge.

Instructions:

NOTE: The halter is made in one piece with two strands of yarn held together.

Using size 11 straight needles and 1 strand of A and B held together, cast on 80 (88, 94, 102 sts). Knit for 3 rows. Work in St st until piece measures 9 (9½, 10, 11)", ending with a p row. K 68 (74, 78, 84). Place last 12 (14, 16, 18) sts on a holder. Turn, p 56 (60, 62, 66) sts, place last 12 (14, 16, 18) sts on a separate holder. Work remaining sts, decreasing 1 st each side as follows: k1, k2tog, work up to last 3 sts, slip 1, k1, psso, k1. Repeat decrease every other row 7 (8, 9, 10) more times. Work even on remaining 40 (42, 42, 44) sts until piece measures 15 (15½, 16, 17)" from start.

MATERIALS:

- ❖ Berroco *Optik* (cotton/acrylic/mohair/metallic/polyester, 87 yds, 50 gm hank)
  Tiffany (#4905), Color A—3 skeins
- ❖ Berroco *Metallica* (rayon/metallic, 85 yds, 25 gm hank)
  Black/Multi (#1012), Color B—3 skeins

- ❖ Size 11/8mm circular needles, 24"

- ❖ Size 11/8mm straight needles

- ❖ 3 stitch holders

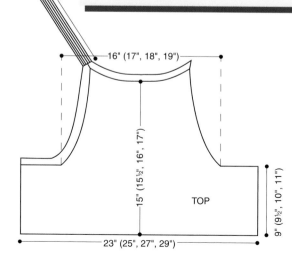

Shape Neckline

K 10 (11, 12, 13) sts, turn, slip first st, bind off slip st and next st. Repeat this decrease every other row 2 more times. (3 sts left). Next row: slip 1, k2tog, psso. Fasten off. Place center 20 sts on holder. Work on remaining 10 (11, 12, 13) sts. Shape other side of neckline to correspond to right side.

Finishing:

Pick up 10 (11, 12, 13) sts at the top of the neckline, the 20 sts from the neckline holder and 10 (11, 12, 13) sts from the other side of the top of the neckline—for a total of 40 (42, 44, 46). Work in garter st (knit all rows) for 4 rows. Bind off from WS.

From RS of armhole, with circular needle, pick up 53 (55, 57, 59) sts, including sts on holder. Cast on an additional 140 (146, 152, 160) sts for strap on right side. Work in garter st on all 193 (201, 209, 219) sts for 4 rows. Bind off from WS.

For left side: Cast on 140 (146, 152, 160) sts for strap on left side, pick up 53 (53, 57, 59) sts from left armhole, including 12 (14, 16, 18) sts on holder. Repeat as for RS. Pick up 34 (36, 38, 40) sts from each side edge of back, knit for 2 rows in garter st. Mark 4 buttonholes evenly spaced between first and last st. To make each buttonhole, bind off 2 sts. In the next row cast on 2 sts. Bind off all sts on 5th row. Slip ties through holes in a criss-cross fashion as shown in picture.

Photo: Christina L. Holmes

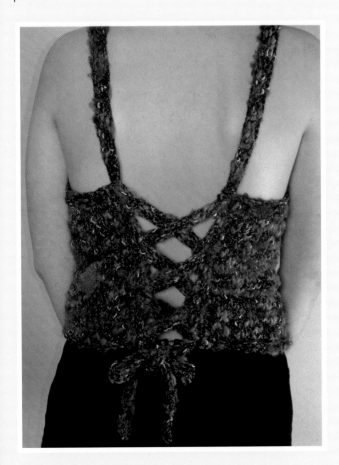

Harlequin Rollneck Pullover

Designed by Joyce Nordstrom for Coats & Clark

Dramatic and elegant, this pullover sweater has a few more twists and turns than other patterns in this book, but once you understand the stitch, it's not that complicated. The subtle diamond pattern is created by purling a stitch from a previous row together with a stitch from the current row on which you are knitting. Initially, the fabric will pucker, giving almost a scalloped look, but as you continue to work the pattern, the knitting will flatten out.

Sizes:

Directions are for women's sizes Extra Small (Small, Medium, Large, X-Large)
Finished bust sizes 36½ (40, 43½ , 47, 50½)"

Gauge:

In Stockinette stitch on larger needles, 7 sts = 3", 6 rows = 2"
To ensure proper fit, take time to check gauge.

NOTE: Bottom of sweater, sleeves and neck have rolled edges in Stockinette stitch rather than ribbing.

Instructions:

Back

Edge: With smaller needles and two double strands of black, cast on 38 (42, 46, 50, 54) sts. K 1 row (mark for RS), (p 1 row, k 1 row) twice; p 1 row, increase 4 sts evenly spaced, 42 (46, 50, 54, 58) sts. Fasten off black. ◇ Change to larger needles.

Pattern:

Row 1: (RS) With MC, k1, p to last st, k1.
Row 2, 4, 6: (WS) p across. Fasten off MC after row 6.
Row 3, 5: Knit across.

MATERIALS:

- ❖ Red Heart® *Light and Lofty*™ (acrylic, 6 oz/148 yd skein)
  Main Color (#9317 Salt & Pepper)— 10 oz
  Color A, Cloud (#9311)—6 oz
  Color B, Onyx (#9312)—6 oz
  Red Heart® *Super Saver* (acrylic, 3 oz/170 yd skein)
  Color C, Black (#312)—2 oz.
  (◇ used double throughout)

- ❖ Size 10½/6.5mm straight knitting needle

- ❖ Size 13/9mm circular knitting needles, 24", or size to obtain gauge

- ❖ Yarn or tapestry needle for finishing

Photo: Christina L. Holmes

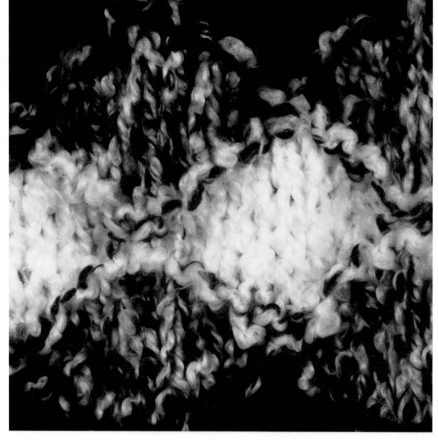

Right side of stitch pattern.

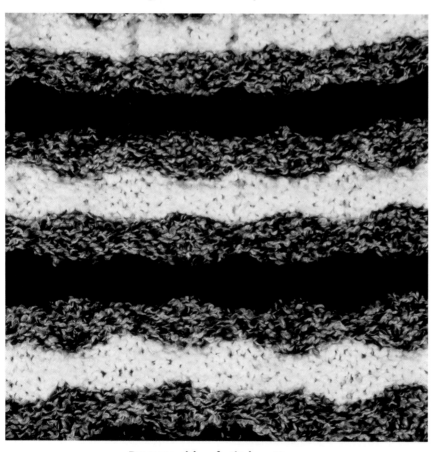

Reverse side of stitch pattern.

Row 7: 🛑 (RS) With A, k1, p0 (2, 0, 2, 0); *p3, [slip next st onto right needle, drop down 6 rows directly below the next st, picking up the front loop of that st, slip both sts onto the left needle and purl them together **(p1 6 sts below)**] twice, p3. Repeat from * to last 1 (3, 1, 3, 1) sts; p0 (2, 0, 2, 0) k1.
Row 8, 10, 12: With A, p across. Fasten off A after row 12.
Row 9, 11: With A, k across
Row 13: (RS) With MC, k1, p0 (2, 0, 2, 0); *p1 6 sts below (see row 7); p6, p1 6 sts below. Repeat from * to last 1 (3, 1, 3, 1) st; p0 (2, 0, 2, 0) k1.
Row 14, 16, 18: With MC, p across. Fasten off MC after row 18.
Row 15, 17: With MC, k across.
Row 19: (RS) With B, repeat row 7.
Row 20, 22, 24: With B, p across. Fasten off B after row 24.
Row 21, 23: With B, k across.
Row 25: (RS) With MC, repeat row 13.

Repeat rows 2–25 for pattern until back measures 20 (20, 20, 22, 22)" or desired length, ending with WS row.

Shoulders

Work in established pattern across 13 (15, 16, 17, 19) sts. Bind off next 16 (18, 18, 20, 20) sts; work in pattern across remaining 13 (15, 16, 17, 19) sts. Next row (WS) bind off. Fasten off. Attach yarn to other shoulder and bind off remaining sts.

Front

Work as for back until piece measures 1½" less than back to shoulders, ending with WS row.

Front Neck

Work in established pattern across 17 (19, 20, 21, 23) sts. Bind off next 8 (10, 10, 12, 12) sts. Work in pattern across remaining 17 (19, 20, 21, 23) sts. Turn. Attaching separate yarn for left shoulder, decrease 1 st at each neck edge on 4 rows. Work even on remaining sts until front measures same as back to shoulder, ending with WS row. Bind off in pattern as for back.

Sleeves

With small needles and two strands of C, cast on 22 (23, 23, 26, 26) sts. K 1 row, (mark for RS), (p 1 row, k 1 row) twice, p 1 row, increase 4 (3, 3, 4, 4) sts evenly across last row, 26 (26, 26, 30, 30) sts. Work as for back to Row 7.

Change to larger needle. **Row 7:** (RS) With A, k1, p0 (0, 0, 2, 2); * p3 **(p1 6 sts below)** twice, p3. Repeat from * to last 1 (1, 1, 3, 3) sts; p 0 (0, 0, 2, 2), k1.

Following pattern for back through row 25, then working in MC St st to end; and working new sts into established pattern, increase 1 st each side of sleeve every 4 rows 4 (4, 4, 4, 4) times; every 6 rows 5 (5, 5, 4, 5) times. When sleeve measures 17 (17½, 17½, 18, 18½)", bind off all sts.

Finishing:

Sew right shoulder seam. With the right side of the sweater facing you, with smaller needles and two strands of C, pick up and k 55 (55, 55, 61, 61) sts around the neck edge. Work in St st for 2", ending with WS row. Bind off all sts loosely. Sew left shoulder seam. Matching center sleeve to shoulder seam, sew sleeves in place. Sew underarm seams. Weave in all loose ends.

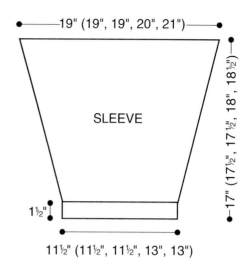

19" (19", 19", 20", 21")

SLEEVE

17" (17½", 17½", 18", 18½")

1½"

11½" (11½", 11½", 13", 13")

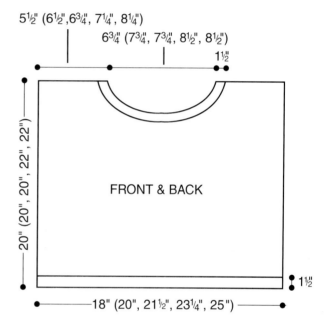

5½" (6½", 6¾", 7¼", 8¼")

6¾" (7¾", 7¾", 8½", 8½")

1½"

FRONT & BACK

20" (20", 20", 22", 22")

1½"

18" (20", 21½", 23¼", 25")

Poncho With Pizzazz

Designed by Berroco Yarns

This striking evening poncho is worked in two strands of metallic ribbon. It's not super fast, but it's a straightforward Stockinette stitch and two simple rectangles. Fringe it or leave it off; you'll still have a style that will have heads turning wherever you go.

Size:

Small. Each panel of the poncho measures 26" x 13" (there are two). To increase a size, add 1" to the length and width for medium, 2" for large, 3" for extra-large and so on. Depending on size, you may need additional yarn.

Gauge:

In Stockinette stitch on size 11 needles, 3½ sts = 1"
To ensure proper fit, take time to check gauge.

Instructions:

▽ **NOTE:** Ribbon yarn may twist as you work with it—don't worry. It doesn't matter!

Make 2 pieces.
With 2 strands of *Metallica* held together, cast on 46 sts. Keeping first and last stitch in garter stitch for selvedge, work even in St st for 26". Bind off.

MATERIALS:

❖ Berroco *Metallica* (rayon/metallic, 25 gm/85 yd hank),
   Silver (#1002)–11 hanks (without fringe), 12 hanks (with fringe)

❖ Size 1⅛mm needles, or size to obtain gauge

❖ Size I/9mm crochet hook

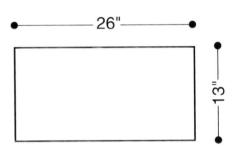

Finishing:

Steam pieces with steam iron and pressing cloth to measurements. Sew cast-on edge of one piece to the first 13" of lower right side edge of second piece. Sew bound-off edge of second piece to first 13" or right lower edge of first piece.

   With crochet hook and 2 strands of *Metallica*, beginning at back point, work one row of single crochet sts around neck edge and outside edge of poncho. Work a second row around neck and outside edge in reverse single crochet. Weave in ends.

Fringe (Optional)

Cut 476, 11" lengths of *Metallica* and working with 4 strands held together and crochet hook, fold in half and draw loop through every other reverse single crochet. Pull through loop and fasten off. Trim fringe if necessary.

Photo: Christina L. Holmes

Cowl Neck Chic

Designed by Arlene Levine

This feathery, hand-dyed yarn works up quickly on size 13 needles into a cowl neck that you can pop over a ho-hum sweater and walk out with instant drama! Remember to keep your eyes on the road with this one: It's easy to set it on cruise control in a straight garter stitch, but don't look away from your stitching or you could easily drop a stitch.

Size: 9" x 24"

Gauge:

3 sts and 3 rows = 1
To ensure proper fit, take time to check your gauge.

▽ *Fluff* is a feathery yarn. To prevent tangling, it is helpful to roll the hank into a ball.
Cast on 27 sts. K each row for 24". Bind off loosely, leaving about 20" length of yarn for seaming. Thread yarn end through yarn or tapestry needle and sew ends together using an overcast stitch.

▽ Do not pull sts too tightly.

▽ If you want to adjust the sizing and knit a longer cowl, it will require a second hank of yarn. An alternative is to make the cowl narrower (7" or 8" instead of 9") which will give you more yarn for the length.

MATERIALS:

❖ Great Adirondack Yarns' *Fluff* (rayon, 82 yd hank), hand-dyed— 1 hank

❖ Size 13/9mm needles, or size to obtain gauge ▽ (We recommend using bamboo needles for this project since the stitches are less likely to slip off.)

❖ Yarn or tapestry needle for finishing

Photo: Christina L. Holmes

Beaded Evening Bag

Designed by Arnetta Kenney

With a subtle sheen to this smooth yarn and some clear "crystal" beads, you've got a great clutch bag that's a little more subdued and versatile than the usual "over-the-top" beaded evening bag. Worked in two strands on size 10 needles, the beading is done as you knit, with the beads threaded onto the yarn in advance, ready to slide forward when needed.

Size: 10" wide by 5" deep

Gauge:

15 stitches = 4".
To ensure the proper size, take time to check your gauge.

Instructions:

NOTE: The bag is knitted with 2 strands of yarn held together.

STOP With 2 strands of yarn held together, thread 24 beads onto the yarn. (Beads will be held "behind" your knitting and when you are ready to position them, you simply bring the bead up to the needle.)

Cast on 38 sts. Work in garter stitch until piece measures 10".

Flap
Row 1: P
Row 2: K2tog, k to last 2 stitches, k2tog—36 sts.
Row 3: P
Row 4: K

STOP **Row 5:** P5. * Bring yarn to back of right hand needle, push 1 bead up close to work, slip the next st purlwise placing bead in front of this stitch. Bring yarn to the front of the right hand needle, purl 5*. Repeat from * to * a total of 5 times. End with p6—5 beads added.
Row 6: Repeat row 2—34 sts.
Row 7-8: Repeat rows 3 and 4.
Row 9: P2. Slip next st, adding a bead (as described in row 5), p4, add a bead on next slip st, * p5, add a bead on next slip st*. Repeat from * to * across row ending with p2—6 beads added.

Row 10: Repeat row 2—32 sts.
Rows 11 – 12: Repeat rows 3 and 4.
Row 13: P4. Add a bead on next slip st, * p5, add a bead on next slip st *. Repeat from * to * across row, ending with P3—5 beads added.
Row 14: Repeat row 2—30 sts
Rows 15 - 16: Repeat Rows 3 and 4.
Row 17: P1, add a bead to next slip st. p4, add a bead to next slip st, * p5, add a bead to next slip st*. Repeat from * to * 2 more times. P3, add a bead to next slip st, p1—6 beads added.
Rows 18 – 21: Knit.

MATERIALS:

❖ Lion Brand *Micro Spun* (microfiber acrylic, 2.5 oz/168 yd balls)
Lilac (#144)—2 balls

❖ Size 10/6 mm knitting needles, or size to obtain gauge

❖ 24 size "E" beads or size with hole large enough to fit over 2 strands of *Micro Spun*

❖ 1 Large decorative button

❖ Needle for threading beads

Bind Off and Button Loop

Bind off 13 sts. With the 2 sts on the right hand needle, and while turning work, work 6 rows of garter stitch (button loop), then continue binding off across the row.

Finishing:

Place knitted fabric flat, RS facing up with loop closure at top. Fold the bottom edge up to the beginning of the flap. Sew side edges with an overcast stitch, matching garter stitch rows. Turn RS out. Fold down flap and sew decorative closure button just below the loop.

Chapter 7

Casual Routes

Classic Button-Front Vest

Designed by Lion Brand Yarn Co.

The texture is the story in this button-front vest. Very light and comfortable to wear, the basic shaping makes it a smooth road to fashion.

Sizes:

Directions are for men's sizes Small (Medium, Large, X-Large) Finished garment at chest measures 44 (46, 48, 50)" Finished garment length: 25½ (25½, 26, 26)"

Gauge:

In Stockinette stitch on size 10 needles, 14 sts and 20 rows = 4¼" To ensure the proper size, be sure to check your gauge

Stitch Pattern:

Ssk = slip, slip, knit: Slip 2 sts knitwise to right hand needle one at a time, insert tip of left hand needle into fronts of these 2 sts and knit them together.

Instructions:

NOTE: All shaping decreases are done inside garter st borders.

Back

With smaller needles, cast on 72 (76, 79, 82) sts. Work in garter st (knit every row) for 6 rows. ◇ Change to larger needles and work in St st until piece measures 14¼" from beginning, end with a RS row.

Establish Garter Armhole Borders

Next row (WS), k7, p to last 7 sts. End k7. Next row (RS): Knit. Continue to work first and last 7 sts in garter st until piece measures 15½" from beginning. End with WS row.

Armhole Shaping

Next row (RS), bind off 3 sts at beginning of row, k to end. Next row (WS), bind off 3 sts at beginning of row, k remaining armhole border sts. P to last 4 sts; end k4. Next row (RS), k4, ssk, k to last 6 sts; end k2tog, k4. 64 (68, 71, 74) sts. Continue to work 4 sts of armhole borders in garter st and rest of row in St st until piece measures 24¼ (24¼, 24¾, 24¾)" from beginning, end with a RS row. Next row (WS), k4, p14 (16, 16, 17), k28 (28, 31, 32), p14 (16, 16, 17), k4. Continue to work first and last 4 sts and center 28 (28, 31, 32) sts in garter st until piece measures 25½ (25½, 26, 26)" from beginning. Bind off all sts.

MATERIALS:

❖ Lion Brand *Homespun* (acrylic/ polyester, 6 oz/185 yd skein) Plantation (#327)—3 (4, 4, 4) balls

❖ Size 9/6mm needles

❖ Size 10/6.5mm, or size needed to obtain the correct gauge

❖ 6, ¾" buttons

❖ Stitch holders

❖ Yarn or tapestry needle for finishing

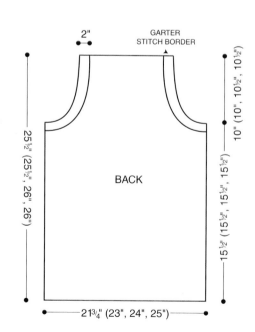

Left Front

With smaller needles, cast on 38 (40, 42, 44) sts. Work in garter st for 4 rows. (STOP) Next (buttonhole) row (RS), K to last 4 sts, k2tog, yo, k2. Continue to work buttonhole row every 16th row 5 times more and AT THE SAME TIME, work 1 more row even in garter st. Next row (RS), change to larger needles and knit row. Next row (WS), k4 (inside edge), p to end. Continue to work as established, working 4 sts of inside edge in garter st and St st over remaining sts until piece measures 14¼" from beginning, end with RS row.

Establish Garter Armhole Borders

Next row (WS), work even to last 7 sts; end k7. Continue to work in pattern established until piece measures 15½" from beginning, end with WS row.

Armhole Shaping

Next row (RS), bind off 3 sts at beginning of row, k rest of row. Next row (WS), p to last 4 sts; end k4. Next row (RS), k4, ssk, k rest of row—34 (36, 38, 40) sts. Continue to work 4 sts of armhole borders in garter st until the piece measures 18½" from beginning, end with a WS row.

Neck Shaping

Next row (RS), continue to work armhole border sts and inside edge sts in garter st. Shape neck as follows: K to last 6 sts, end with k2tog. K to end. P next row. Repeat last 2 rows 11 (11, 13, 14) times more—22 (24, 24, 25) sts. Work even until piece measures same length as back. Bind off all sts.

Right Front

With smaller needles, cast on 38 (40, 42, 44) sts. Work in garter st for 6 rows. Next row (RS), change to larger needles and knit row. Next row (WS), p to last 4 sts, end k4 (inside edge). Continue to work in pattern established, working 4 sts of inside edge in garter st and St st over remaining sts, until piece measures 14¼" from beginning, end with RS row.

Establish Garter Armhole Borders

Next row (WS), k7, p to end of row. Continue to work in pattern established until piece measures 15½" from beginning, end with a RS row. (CAUTION) Armhole Shaping Next row (WS), bind off 3 sts at beginning of row, k remaining armhole border sts, purl to end of row. Next row (RS), knit to last 6 sts; end k2tog, k4. 34 (36, 38, 40) sts. Continue to work 4 sts of armhole borders in garter st and rest of row in St st until piece measures 18½" from beginning, end with a WS row.

Neck Shaping

Next row (RS), continue to work armhole border sts and inside edge sts in garter st, shape neck as follows. Work 4 sts, ssk, work rest of row even. Work 1 row even. Repeat last 2 rows 11 (11, 13, 14) times more—22 (24, 24, 25) sts. Work even until piece measures same length as back. Bind off all sts.

Finishing:

Sew shoulder and side seams. Block all pieces lightly. Sew buttons opposite buttonholes.

Photo: Mary Colucci

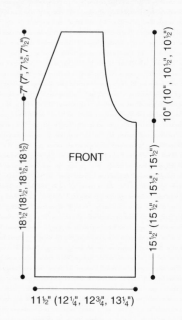

7" (7, 7½, 7½")

10" (10, 10½, 10½")

18½" (18½, 18½, 18½")

FRONT

15½" (15½, 15½, 15½")

11½" (12¼, 12¾, 13¼")

Tweedy V-Neck Vest

Designed by Lion Brand Yarn Co.

Here's a classic tweed vest that any man would enjoy wearing. Perfect for casual Fridays, the alpaca blend yarn adds a touch of luxury. Working with two strands of different colored yarns creates the tweed effect. Try it in your man's favorite color combinations.

Sizes:

Directions are for men's size Small (Medium, Large, X-Large) Finished chest sizes 42 (44, 46, 48)"

Gauge:

In Stockinette stitch on size 10½ needles, 13 sts and 16 rows = 4" To ensure the proper fit, take time to check your gauge.

Stitch Pattern:

Ssk = slip, slip, knit: Slip 2 sts knitwise to right hand needle one at a time, insert tip of left hand needle into fronts of these 2 sts and knit them together.

MATERIALS:

❖ Lion Brand AL•PA•KA
   (wool/alpaca/acrylic, 1.75-oz/
   107 yd skein)
   Black (#153), Color A—
   5 (6, 6, 7) skeins
   Oxford Grey (#152), Color B—
   5 (6, 6, 7) skeins

❖ Size 9/5.5mm knitting needles

❖ Size 10½/6.50mm knitting needles

❖ Size 9/5.5mm 16" circular needles,
   or size needed to obtain gauge

❖ Stitch holders

❖ Stitch markers

❖ Yarn or tapestry needle for finishing

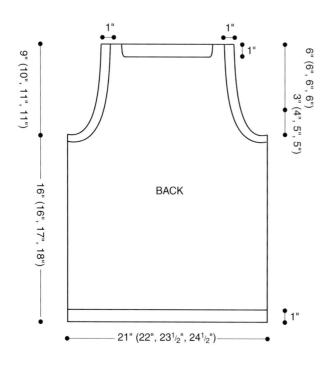

Instructions:

Back

NOTE: Vest is made holding 2 strands of yarn together throughout.

With size 9 needle and a strand of Color A and Color B held together, cast on 68 (72, 76, 80) sts. Work in garter st (k all rows) for 6 rows.

⬥ Change to size 10 1/2 needles. Continue in St st until piece measures 16 (16, 17, 18)" from beginning, end with p row.

Armhole Shaping

Bind off 5 sts at beginning of next 2 rows. Decrease row (RS): K2, ssk, knit to last 4 sts, k2tog, k2. Repeat decreases 6 (7, 8, 9) times more—44 (46, 48, 50) sts. Work even until armhole measures 9 (10, 11, 11)". Bind off 6 sts at beginning of next 2 rows. Bind off 5 (5, 6, 6) sts at beginning of next 2 rows. Place remaining 22 (24, 24, 26) sts onto stitch holder for back neck.

Front

Work as for back until armhole measures 3 (4, 5, 5)". End with p row. Place marker in the middle of work. Continue armhole shaping and at the same time shape V-neck.

V-Neck Shaping

Knit to last 3 sts before marker, k2tog, k1. Attach two separate strands of Color A and B to other side and knit remaining sts as follows: k1, ssk, work to the end. Work both sides of the V-Neck at the same time. Next row: P. Repeat these two rows 10 (11, 11, 12) times more. When armholes measure same as back, bind off 6 sts at beginning of next 2 rows. Bind off 5 (5, 6, 6) sts at beginning of next 2 rows.

Finishing:

Neck

Sew shoulders together. With RS facing and circular needle knit across 22 (24, 24, 26) sts from back holder, pick up along left side V-Neck 3 sts from every 4 rows, 1 st from the middle, pick up along right side V-Neck 3 sts from every 4 rows, join, work in round. Next round: p, decrease 2 sts in the middle V-Neck as follows: p3tog (take 1 st from left side, 1 central st, 1 st from right side). Repeat decreases in every round. Purl 3 more rounds. Bind off purlwise.

Armbands

Sew side seams. With RS facing and circular needle pick up 4 sts from back underarm, pick up along back and front armholes 3 sts from every 4 rows, pick up 4 sts from front underarm, place marker, join, work in round. Next round: P, decrease 1 st after marker, 1 st before marker (p2tog). Repeat decreases in every round. P 3 more rounds. Bind off purlwise.
Weave in loose ends. Lightly steam.

Photo: Christina L. Holmes

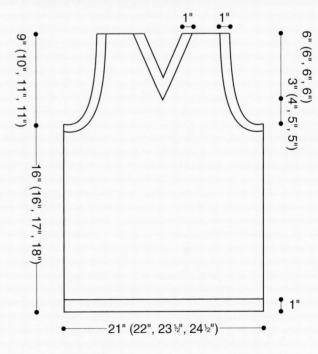

Zippy Vest

Designed by Brenda Lewis for Coats & Clark

The zippered vest is a jazzier version of an old favorite. The slip stitch pattern adds a rich texture and two strands of yarn on size 13 needles ensure that it will zip along too!

Sizes:

Directions are for men's sizes Small (Medium, Large)
Finished chest sizes 40 (44, 47)"
Finished length 25 (25½, 27½)"

Gauge:

With size 13 needles in pattern, 5 sts and 8 rows = 2"
To ensure proper fit, take time to check your gauge

Pattern Stitch:

Row 1: K1, *yarn front, slip one purlwise, yarn back, k1, rep from * to end of row.
Row 2: Purl

Instructions:

NOTE: Vest is made holding 2 strands of yarn together throughout.

Back

With size 11 needles and 2 strands A, cast on 51 (55, 59) sts. Work in ribbing as follows: **Row 1 (RS):** K1, *p1, k1; repeat from * across. **Row 2:** P1, *k1, p1; repeat from * across. Repeat rows 1 and 2 for 2½", increasing 2 sts evenly on last row, end row 2—53 (57, 61) sts. Change to larger needles and work in even pattern until 14" from beginning, ending WS row. Bind off 2 (2, 3) sts at the beginning of the next 2 rows, 49 (53, 55) sts. Decrease 1 st each end of row every RS row 2 times. Work even in established pattern until back measures 25 (25½, 27½)", ending with a WS row. If you are going to sew the shoulder seams, bind off all sts. If you are going to sew the shoulder seams, work 13 (14, 15) sts and slip to holder, bind off the next 19 (21, 21) sts for back neck, work remaining sts and slip to holder.

MATERIALS:

- Red Heart® *Super Saver* (acrylic, 8 oz/348 yd skein),
  Denim Heather (#408), Color A—
  2 skeins
  Buff Fleck (# 4334), Color B—
  1 skein

- Size 11/8mm knitting needles

- Size 13/9mm knitting needles, or size to obtain gauge

- Size N/15 crochet hook

- Size 14" sweater/ jacket separating zipper for small and medium; size 16" for size large

- Beige sewing thread and sewing needle

- Yarn or tapestry needle for finishing

- Stitch holders (optional)

Left Front

With size 11 needles and 2 strands A, cast on 25 (27, 29) sts. Work ribbing same as for back, including increase— 27 (29, 31). Change to size 13 needles and work even in pattern until 14", ending with WS row.

◈ Sizes small and medium only: Decrease 1 st at the neck edge next row then every other row 1 time, then every 4th row 8 (9) times. At the same time, when front measures 15", ending with a WS row bind off 2 sts at the armhole edge, then decrease 1 st at armhole edge every RS row 2 times.

Size large only: Continue in pattern until front measures 16", ending with a WS row. Bind off 3 sts at the armhole edge, decrease 1 st at the neck edge. Decrease 1 st at the neck edge every other row 1 time, then every 4th row 9 times. At the same time, decrease 1 st at the armhole edge every RS row 2 times.

Work even on 13 (14, 15) sts until front measures 25 (25½, 27½)", ending with a WS row. Bind off sts if sewing shoulders, slip sts onto holder if weaving the shoulder seams together.

Right Front

Work the same as left front, reversing neck and armhole shaping.

Finishing:

Sew together shoulder seams. Sew side seams.

Front and Neckband

With RS facing, using size N crochet hook and 2 strands of Color B, begin at the bottom edge of right front and work 1 sc into the first st, * skip the next st, 1 sc into the next st, repeat from * to bottom edge of left front. Ch 1, work 1 reverse sc into each st around. Fasten off.

Armhole Band

With RS facing, using Size N crochet hook and 2 strands of Color B, work 1 sc into the first st, * skip 1 st, work 1 sc into the next st. Join with a slip st in beginning sc. Ch 1, work 1 reverse sc into each st around. Join with a slip st.

Fasten off.

Weave in yarn ends.

Pin zipper to front bands between bottom edge and first neck shaping decrease. Sew by hand.

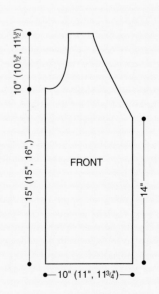

Photo: Christina L. Holmes

Chapter 8

Hey Baby!
For the Car Seat Set

Salt & Pepper Sweater & Hat

Designed by Kathleen Sams for Coats & Clark

Textured, flecked yarn creates a beautiful tweedy look in this sophisticated baby cardigan with matching hat, and fun buttons like the "puppy" design shown here add a whimsical touch. The best part is that the body is knitted in one piece for minimal finishing.

Sizes:

Directions are for 3 mos (6, 9, 12, 18) mos

Gauge:

In pattern stitch on 15 needles, 8 sts and 12 rows = 4"
To ensure proper fit, take time to check your gauge.

Garter Fleck Stripe Pattern

Row 1 (RS): With A, k3, * p3, k3; repeat from * across.
Row 2: Repeat Row 1.
Row 3: With B, k3, * p3, k3; repeat from * across.
Row 4: Repeat row 3.
Repeat these 4 rows for pattern.

Instructions:

Body (Worked in one piece to underarms)

With size 13 needles and B cast on 33 (39, 45, 51, 57) sts. K 4 rows. Change to size 15 needles and work in pattern stitch until 5 (5½, 6, 6½, 7)" from beginning, end row 4.

Divide for Front and Back

Keeping continuity of stripe pattern, work across 7 (9, 11, 13, 15) sts; turn and put remaining sts on a holder. Work even on these sts until 3½ (4, 4, 4½, 4½)" above division.

Neck Shaping

Decrease 1 st at neck edge on next 2 (2, 3, 4, 5) rows. Bind off.

MATERIALS:

❖ Red Heart® *Light & Lofty*™ (acrylic, 6 oz/148 yd skein)
   Salt & Pepper (#9317), Color A— 1 (1, 2, 2, 2) skeins
   Onyx (#9312) Color B—1 skein

❖ Size 13/9mm circular knitting needles, 16"

❖ Size 15/10mm circular knitting needles, 16", or size to obtain gauge

❖ Stitch holders

❖ 4 or 5, ⅝" to 1" buttons

❖ Yarn or tapestry needle for finishing

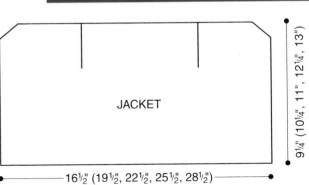

JACKET

9¼" (10¼", 11", 12¼", 13")

16½" (19½", 22½", 25½", 28½")

Back

With RS facing, join yarn to last long row and work in pattern across 19 (21, 23, 25, 27) sts. Work even in pattern stitch on these sts until back measures same as right front to shoulder. Bind off.

Left Front

With RS facing, join yarn to remaining sts. Complete to correspond to right front, reversing neck shaping.

Sleeves

With size 13 needles and B cast on 11 (11, 13, 13, 15) sts. K 4 rows. Increase 5 (5, 7, 7, 7) sts evenly spaced across next row.

▽ Change to larger needles and work in pattern stitch, shaping sides by increasing 1 st each end of 3rd row, then every other row to 23 (23, 25, 25, 27) sts. Work even until 6½ (7, 7, 7½, 8)" from beginning. Bind off.

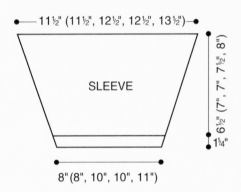

11½" (11½", 12½", 12½", 13½")

SLEEVE

6½" (7", 7", 7½", 8")

1¼"

8" (8", 10", 10", 11")

Photo: Christina L. Holmes

Finishing:

Sew shoulder seams. With RS of sweater and sleeves facing, set in sleeves and sew in armholes. Sew sleeve seams.

Neckband

With RS facing, size 13 needles and B, pick up and k4 (4, 5, 6, 6) sts across right front, 10 (12, 14, 16, 16) sts across back, 4 (4, 5, 6, 6) across left front. K4 rows. Bind off.

Front Bands

With RS facing, size 13 needles and B, pick up and k23 (25, 27, 29, 31) sts. K 4 rows. Bind off.

Sew on buttons, evenly spaced—left side for girls, right side for boys.

NOTE: There is no need to make separate buttonholes. Buttons slip easily through the bulky, textured yarn. The number of buttons you use will depend on the size sweater you make and the size button you select.

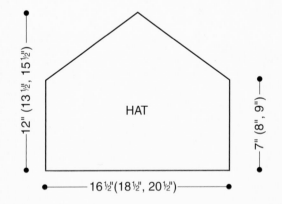

12" (13 ½", 15 ½")

HAT

7" (8", 9")

16½" (18½", 20½")

Hat

With size 13 needles and A cast on 33 (37, 41) sts. Work in pattern as for cardigan body until 7 (8, 9)" from beginning.

Shape Top

Decrease 1 st each end of every other row until 3 sts remaining. K 1 row. Cut yarn leaving a long end for sewing. Thread yarn into a yarn needle and through remaining sts. Draw up tightly and fasten securely. Sew back seam. Knot top of hat to fit.

Cable Sweat Suit

Designed by Bernat Design Studio

Racing stripes accent the grey ragg in this child's raglan-sleeved sweat suit with a buttoned shoulder and single front cable. This is one project that requires you to slow down and read through the instructions, so that you will recognize the changes that occur in shaping. It is one of the more difficult patterns in this book, but as a child's design, it's small in size! The accent colors shown are basically unisex: try a bright aqua or hot pink for a girl, and consider doing the front cable in one of the bright accents.

Sizes:

Children 6 mos (12 mos, 18 mos, 2 yrs, 4 yrs)
Finished chest sizes 20 (22, 25, 26, 29)"

Gauge:

With size 7 needles and Stockinette stitch, 19 sts and 24 rows = 4"
To ensure proper fit, take time to check your gauge.

Patterns:

Cable

Panel Pattern A (worked over 8 sts)
Row 1: (RS) P1, k6, p1.
Row 2 and even rows: K1, p6, k1.
Row 3: P1, slip next 3 sts onto a cable needle and leave at back of work, k3, then k3 from cable needle (C6B), p1.
Row 5 and 7: Same as row 1.
Row 8: Same as row 2.
Repeat rows 1-8 for panel pattern A.

Stripe

20 rows form stripe pattern:
With A, work 4 rows in St st.
With MC, work 4 rows in St st.
With B, work 4 rows in St st.
With MC, work 4 rows in St st.
With C, work 4 rows in St st.

MATERIALS:

❖ Bernat's *Berella* 4 (acrylic, 3.5 oz/ 100 gm ball)
  Grey Ragg (#10078), Main Color (MC)—3 (4, 5, 5, 6) balls
  Dark Oxford (#8893), Color A—1 (1, 1, 1, 1) ball
  Navy (#8965), Color B—1 (1, 1, 1, 1) ball
  Light Tapestry Gold (#8886), Color C—1 (1, 1, 1, 1) ball

❖ Sizes 5/3.75mm knitting needles

❖ 7/4.5mm knitting needles, or size needed to obtain tension

❖ 3, ⅝" buttons

❖ Cable needle

❖ 4 stitch holders

❖ Elastic for waist

❖ Yarn or tapestry needle for finishing

❖ Bobbins (optional)

Instructions for Suit Top:

Back

With size 5 needles and A, cast on 41 (45, 51, 55, 61) sts.

Row 1: (RS) K1. * p1, k1, repeat from * to end of row.

Row 2: P1, * k1, p1, repeat from * to end of row.

Repeat these 2 rows of (k1, p1) ribbing for 2", increasing 5 sts evenly across last row, 46 (50, 56, 60, 66) sts.

⬥ Change to MC, size 7 needles and proceed in St st until piece measures 6 (6½, 7, 8, 9)" from beginning, ending with RS row.

Shape Raglans

Bind off 2 sts at beginning of next 2 rows, 42 (46, 52, 56, 62) sts.

Next row: (RS) K1, slip 1, k1, psso. Knit to last 3 sts, k2tog. k1.

Next row: Purl.

Repeat last 2 rows 13 (15, 15, 15, 15) more times. 14 (14, 20, 24, 30) sts.

⬥ Sizes 6, and 18 months, 2 yrs and 4 yrs only: **Next row:** (RS) K1, slip 1, k1, psso. Knit to last 3 sts, k2tog, k1.

Next row: P1, p2tog, p to last 3 sts, p2tog through the back loop of the stitch, p1.

Repeat last 2 rows 0 (0, 1, 1, 2) time(s) more.

All sizes: Leave remaining 10 (14,16,16,18) sts on a st holder.

Photo: Christina L. Holmes

Front

🛑 **NOTE:** When introducing a different color yarn in the middle of the row, it is helpful to use yarn bobbins or to wind small balls of the colors to be used, one for each separate area of color in the design. Start new colors at appropriate points. To change colors, bring the color you have been working with to the left on the WS and pick up the new color from under it or twist the two colors around each other where they meet, on WS, to avoid a hole.

With smaller needles and A, cast on 41 (45, 51, 55, 61) sts.

Work in (k1, p1) ribbing for 2" as given for back, increase 7 sts evenly across last row, 48 (52, 58, 62, 68) sts.

⬥ Change to size 7 needles and proceed as follows:

Row 1: (RS) With MC, k10 (14, 16, 18, 20). With A, work first row of panel pattern A (See Cable Pattern) across next 8 sts. With MC, knit to end of row.

Row 2: With MC, p 30 (30, 34, 36, 40). With A, work 2nd row of panel pattern A across next 8 sts. With MC, p to end of row. These 2 rows form pattern.

Continue in pattern until work from beginning measures same length as back before raglan shaping, ending with RS facing.

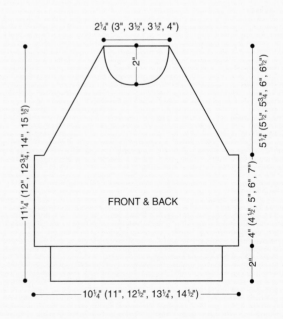

2¼" (3", 3½", 3½", 4")

2"

11¼" (12", 12¾", 14", 15 ½")

5¼" (5½", 5¾", 6", 6½")

FRONT & BACK

4" (4½", 5", 6", 7")

2"

10¼" (11", 12½", 13¼", 14½")

Shape Raglans

Bind off 2 sts at beginning of next 2 rows, 44 (48, 54, 58, 64) sts.

Next row: (RS) k1, slip 1, k1, psso. Continue panel pattern to last 3 sts, k2tog, k1.

Next row: Work even in pattern.

Repeat last 2 rows 7 (8, 9, 10, 11) more times. 28 (30, 34, 36, 40) sts.

Neck Shaping

Row 1: (RS) K1, slip 1, k1, psso, panel pattern across 8 sts. Turn. Leave remaining sts on a stitch holder.

Row 2: P2tog. Work panel pattern to end of row. Decrease 1 st at raglan edge on next and every other row and **at the same time** decrease 1 st at neck edge on next 3 rows.

Decrease 1 st at raglan edge as you did for the back until there are 3 sts.

Next row: (RS) Slip 1, k1, psso, k1.

Next row: P2.

Next row: Slip 1, k1, psso. Fasten off.

With RS of work facing, slip next 4 (6, 10, 12 ,16) sts on a stitch holder. Join MC to remaining sts and knit to last 3 sts. K2tog, k1.

Next row: Continue panel pattern to last 2 sts, p2tog through the back loop.

Decrease 1 st at raglan edge on next and following alternate row at the same time decrease 1 st at neck edge on next 3 rows.

Decrease 1 st at raglan edge as given for back until there are 3 sts.

Next row: K1, k2tog.

Next row: P2.

Next row: K2tog, fasten off.

Sleeves

With size 5 needles and A, cast on 29 (29, 29, 35, 35) sts. Work 2" in (kl, p1) ribbing as you did for back, increase 1 st at center of last row and ending with RS facing for next row, 30 (30, 30, 36, 36) sts.

Change to size 7 needles and MC and work 2 rows in Stst increasing 1 st each end of needle on next and every other row to 32 (32, 36, 38, 38) sts.

Begin stripe pattern and increase 1 st each end of row every 2 (2, 4, 4, 4) rows, 42 (46, 50, 52, 56) sts. After completing the stripe pattern once, with MC, continue even in St st until sleeve measures 6½ (7, 7½, 8, 8½)" from beginning, ending with RS facing for next row.

Shape Raglans

Bind off 2 sts beginning next 2 rows, 38 (42, 46, 48, 52) sts.

Next row: (RS) k1, slip 1, k1, psso, knit to last 3 sts, k2tog, k1.

Next row: Purl.

Repeat last 2 rows 12 (13, 13, 15, 15) times more. 12 (14, 18, 16, 20) sts.

Next row: (RS) K1, slip 1, k1, psso, knit to last 3 sts, k2tog, k1.

Next row: P1, p2tog, purl to last 3 sts, p2tog through the back loop, p1.

Repeat last 2 rows 1 (1, 2, 1, 2) more time(s). Leave remaining 4 (6, 6, 8, 8) sts on a stitch holder.

Finishing:

Neckband

Sew raglan seams leaving back left raglan open. With RS of work facing, A and size 5 needles, K4 (6, 6, 8, 8) from left sleeve stitch holder. Pick up and knit 8 sts down left neck edge. K4 (6, 10, 12, 16) from front stitch holder. Pick up and knit 8 sts up right front neck edge. K4 (6, 6, 8, 8) from right sleeve stitch holder. K10 (14, 16, 16, 18) from back-stitch holder, decrease (k2tog) 1 st at center back, 37 (47, 55, 59, 65) sts.

Work in (k1, p1) ribbing as worked for the back for 2½", ending with RS facing for next row. Bind off loosely in ribbing. ▽ (This ribbing will later be folded over to form the collar.)

Fold neckband in half to WS and sew in position. Sew right back raglan seam leaving neckband and upper 2" of raglan seam open.

With RS of work facing, pick up and knit 13 sts along seam opening and side of neckband, working through both thickness. Work 1 row in k1, p1 ribbing as given for back.

Next row: (buttonhole row) Rib (k1, p1) 3 sts. [Bind off 2 sts. Rib 3 sts (including st after bind off)] twice.

Next row: Rib across the row (k1, p1), casting on 2 sts above bind off sts.

Next row: Work in ribbing even. Bind off in ribbing. Sew side and sleeve seams. Sew on buttons to correspond to buttonholes.

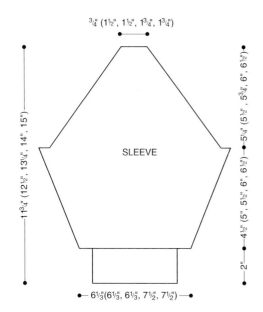

¾" (1½", 1½", 1¾", 1¾")

1-¾" (12½", 13¾, 14", 15")

4½" (5", 5½", 6", 6½")

—5¼" (5½", 5¾, 6", 6½")

SLEEVE

2"

6⅓"(6⅓, 6⅓", 7½", 7½")

structions for Sweat Pants:

ght Leg (beginning at waist)
With size 7 needles and MC, cast on 54 (57, 60, 62, sts.

w 1: (RS) K1, *p1, k1. Repeat from * to end of row.
w 2: P1, *k1, p1. Repeat from * to end of row.
eat these 2 rows (k1, p1) ribbing for 2¼" ending on a row.**

ceed as follows:

ape Back
t 2 rows: K10. Turn. Slip 1 purlwise, purl to end of row.
t 2 rows: K18. Turn. Slip 1 purlwise. Purl to end of row.
t 2 rows: K26. Turn. Slip 1 purlwise. Purl to end of row.
t 2 rows: K34. Turn. Slip 1 purlwise. Purl to end of row.
t 2 rows: K42. Turn. Slip 1 purlwise. Purl to end of row.

NOTE: To avoid a hole when knitting a slipped stitch,
up the st below the slipped st and slip it onto left-
d needle. Knit this st together with the slip st above.
tinue in St st until work from center front measures
¼, 8½, 9¼, 10)", ending with RS facing for next row.

*Shape Crotch
tinue in St st as established, increasing 1 st each end
ext and following 0 (0, 0, 1,1) every other row(s).
t on 2 sts beginning of next 2 rows. 60 (63, 66, 70,
sts.
k 2 rows even.

ape Inseam
tinue in pattern, decreasing 1 st each end of needle
ext and every other row until there are 44 (51, 56,
58) sts, then on following 4th rows until there are 32
38, 40, 40) sts.
tinue even in St st until work from last cast on at
ch measures approximately 7¼ (7¾, 8¼, 9¼, 9¾)", end-
with RS facing for next row.
nge to size 5 needles and A and work 6 rows in (k1,
ribbing. Bind off in ribbing.***

Left Leg (beginning at waist)
Work from ** to ** as for right leg.
Proceed as follows, noting that first row is WS:

Shape Back
Next 2 rows: P10. Turn. Slip 1 knitwise, knit to end of row.
Next 2 rows: P18. Turn. Slip 1 knitwise, knit to end of row.
Next 2 rows: P26. Turn. Slip 1 knitwise, knit to end of row.
Next 2 rows: P34. Turn. Slip 1 knitwise, knit to end of row.
Next 2 rows: P42. Turn. Slip 1 knitwise, knit to end of row.

▽ **NOTE:** To avoid a hole when purling a slipped st, pick
up the st below the slipped st and slip it onto left-hand
needle. Purl this st tog with the slipped st above.
Next row: P across all sts.
Proceed in St st until work from center front measures
8 (8¼, 8½, 9¼, 10)", ending with RS facing for next row.
Work from *** to *** as for right leg.

Finishing:
Sew inseams. Sew crotch seam. Fold waistband in half to
wrong side and sew loosely in position leaving an opening
to insert elastic. Cut elastic to waist measurement and
insert through waistband. Sew ends of elastic together
securely. Sew opening of waistband closed.

Color Block Sweater

Designed by Kathleen Sams for Coats & Clark

With three strands of yarn and large-size needles, you'll finish this colorful front-zippered cardigan so quickly you may get a ticket for speeding! That's the fun of knitting infant and children's projects—the small size makes it manageable!

Sizes:

Children's sizes Small (Medium, Large)
Finished Chest size, 26 (28, 30)"
Finished length: 14 (16, 17)"

Gauge:

In Stockinette stitch with size 15 needles and three strands of yarn held together, 10 sts and 13 rows = 4"
To ensure proper fit, take time to check your gauge.

Instructions:

NOTE: Work with 3 strands held together as one throughout.

Back

With 2 strands of B and 1 strand A, cast on 33 (35, 38) sts. K4 rows. Work in St st (k1 row, p1 row) until piece measures 13½ (15½, 16½)", ending p row.

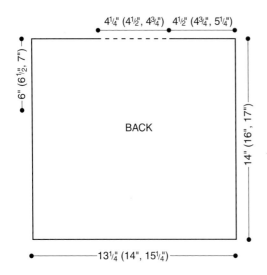

MATERIALS:

❖ Red Heart® *Kids*™ (acrylic, 5 oz/302 yd solid and 4 oz/242 yd multi-color skeins)
   Blue (#2845), Color A—3 (6, 6) skeins
   Crayon (#2930), Color B—3 (3, 3) skeins
   Green (#2677), Color C—3 (3, 3) skeins
   Red (#2390), Color D—3 skeins

❖ Size 15/10mm knitting needles or size to obtain gauge

❖ Separating zipper **NOTE:** Zipper length depends on sweater size. We used a 15" zipper length for the medium-size sweater.)

❖ Stitch holders

❖ Stitch markers

❖ Yarn or tapestry needle for finishing

Neck Shaping

Row 1: K9 (10, 11), k2tog, slip remaining sts on a holder. **Row 2:** P. Bind off.
Leave center 11 (11, 12) sts on holder. With RS facing, pick up remaining 11 (12, 13) sts. Complete to correspond to neck shaping of first side, reversing shaping.

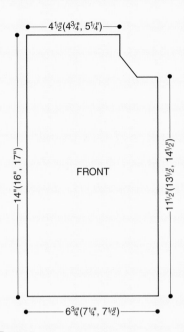

FRONT

4½"(4¾", 5¼")

14"(16", 17")

11½"(13½", 14½")

6¾"(7¼", 7½")

Photo: Christina L. Holmes

Right Front

With 3 strands of A, cast on 15 (16, 18) sts. K4 rows. ⬦CAUTION Change to 3 strands C and work in St st until piece measures 6 (7, 8)". ⬦CAUTION Change to 3 strands of B and continue in St st until piece measures 11½ (13½, 14½)".

Neck Shaping

Bind off 3 sts at beginning of next row. Decrease 1 st at neck edge every right side row 2 (2, 3) times. Work even until piece measures 14 (16, 17)" ending wrong side row. Bind off.

Left Front

With 3 strands of A, cast on 15 (16, 18) sts. K 4 rows. ⬦CAUTION Change to 3 strands of D and work in St st until piece measures 8 (9, 10)". ⬦CAUTION Change to 3 strands of A and work even until piece measures 11½ (13½, 14½)". Complete as to correspond to first side, reversing shaping. Bind off.

Sleeves (Make 2)

Sew front and back shoulder seams. Place markers 6 (6½, 7)" below shoulder seams on front and back. With right side facing and 3 strands of A, pick up and k30 (32, 35) sts between markers. Working in garter st (k each row), decrease 1 st each end on 8th row, then every 6th row 3 times. Work even on 24 (26, 29) sts until piece measures approximately 11 (13, 14)". Bind off.

Finishing:

Neckband

With RS facing and 3 strands of A, pick up and K13 sts along the right neck edge, 11 (11, 12) sts from the back holder, and 13 sts along the left neck edge— 37 (37, 38) sts. Knit 1 row, k10 (10, 11), k2tog, k13 (13, 12), k2tog, k10 (10, 11)—35 (35, 36) sts. Knit 1 row. Bind off.

Sew side and sleeve seams. Sew zipper in place under front edge. Weave in ends.

12" (12¾", 14")

SLEEVE

11" (13", 14")

9½" (10½", 11½")

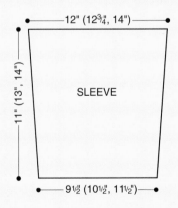

▽ TIP: We recommend hand stitching the zipper. Machine sewing can warp or rip the fabric.

Girl's Tank Top

Designed by Brenda Lewis for Coats & Clark

Shoulder-tied straps give a fun touch to this child's summer tank top. The front and back are worked in one piece and finished with a single crochet trim on the neck and arms.

Sizes:

Directions are for girl's sizes Small (Medium, Large, X-Large)
Finished garment at chest measures 26½ (28½, 31, 33)"
Length: 13 (13½, 14, 15)"

Gauge:

In Stockinette stitch, using size 7 needle,
    9 sts and 12 rows = 2"
To ensure the proper fit, take time to check your gauge.

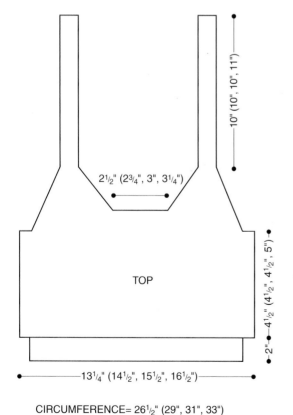

2½" (2¾", 3", 3¼")

10" (10", 10", 11")

TOP

4½" (4½", 4½", 5")

2"

13¼" (14½", 15½", 16½")

CIRCUMFERENCE= 26½" (29", 31", 33")

MATERIALS:

- ❖ Aunt Lydia's® *Denim* (cotton/acrylic, 400 yd ball)
  Rose (#1026)—1 ball

- ❖ Size 5/3.75mm circular needles

- ❖ Size 7/4.5mm circular knitting needles, or size needed to obtain gauge

- ❖ 2 double pointed knitting needles, size 6

- ❖ Size H crochet hook

- ❖ 2 stitch holders

- ❖ 2 stitch markers

Instructions:

Using size 5 circular needles, cast on 120 (130, 140, 150) sts. **STOP** Spread your stitches along the length of the needle, making sure they are not twisted. Hold needle end with cast on stitches in the left hand, place marker over right hand needle point and work the first stitch on the left-hand point, pulling yarn firmly to prevent a gap. Work k1, p1 ribbing over 60 (65, 70, 75) sts, place 2nd marker on needle. Work around to the marker to complete one round. Slip the marker and continue with the next round and work k1, p1 ribbing in rounds for 2 inches, pulling yarn firmly at beginning of each round. **CAUTION** Change to size 7 needle and k in rounds until piece measures 6½ (6½, 6½, 7)".

Divide for front and back:

Next row * k to the last 4 sts before marker, bind off 4 sts before marker, remove marker and bind off next 4 sts, repeat from *. K to end of row. Slip the first 52 (57, 62, 67) sts worked onto holder for front. Working in rows on 52 (57, 62, 67) sts for back, work in St st and decrease 1 st each end of needle every right side row 3 (4, 4, 5) times. 46 (49, 54, 57) sts on needle.

Neck Shaping

Next row k17 (18, 20, 21) sts and slip onto holder for right shoulder, bind off next 12 (13, 14, 15) sts for neck back, k next 17 (18, 20, 21) sts for left shoulder. Work in St st and decrease 1 st each end of the needle every RS row 7 (7, 8, 9) times, 3 (4, 4, 3) sts on needle. P one row.

⬦Sizes Medium and Large: only next row decrease 1 st, purl one row.

Straps

Slip 3 sts onto size 6 double pointed needle and work as follows: k3, * slip sts to opposite end of needle and holding thread firmly, k3. Repeat from * until strap measures 10 (10, 11, 11)". Bind off.

Slip sts for back right shoulder onto size 7 needle and work the same as for left shoulder. Slip sts for front onto size 7 needle and work the same as for back.

Finishing:

Underarms

With RS facing using size H crochet hook, work 1 sc into first st below strap, * skip 1 st, work 1 sc into the next st, repeat from * to the strap. Fasten off.

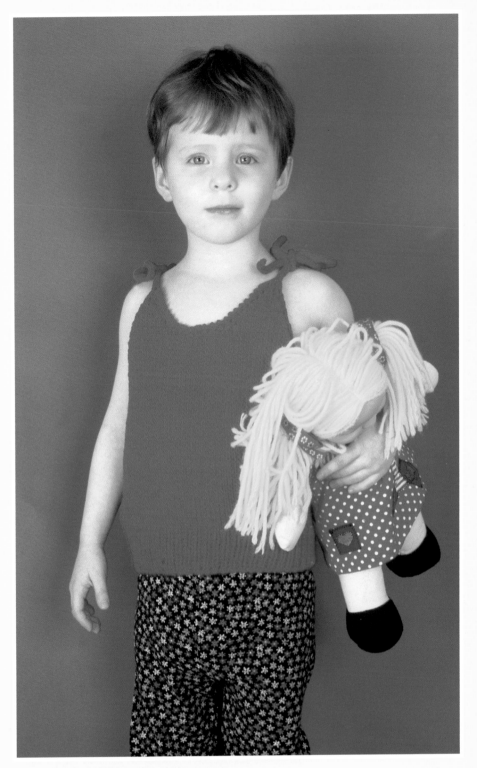

Photo: Christina L. Holmes

Neck

With right side facing, work 1 sc into the first st below strap, *skip the next st, work 1 sc into the next st, repeat from * to the strap, ch 1, work 1 reverse sc into each st across. Fasten off. Weave in yarn ends.

Broken-Cable Afghan

Designed by Bernat Design Studio

Whether in the car seat or crib, your favorite baby will be cruising to dreamland wrapped in this soft and light afghan. Once you master the broken cable pattern, you'll want to make an afghan for yourself, too!

Size:

Baby, 31 by 39"
(Adult, 43 by 57")

Gauge:

In Stockinette stitch with size 15 needle, 9 sts and 14 rows = 4"

Stitch Patterns:

C6B = slip next 3 sts onto a cable needle and leave at back of work. K3, then k3 from cable needle.

C6F = slip next 3 sts onto a cable needle and leave at front of work. K3, then k3 from cable needle.

MATERIALS:

❖ Bernat *Breeze* (acrylic/nylon,140 gm/178 yd balls)
 Seafoam (#106)
 Baby size—5 balls
 Full size—9 balls

❖ Size 15/10mm circular knitting needle, 24", or size to obtain gauge

❖ Cable needle

❖ Yarn or tapestry needle for finishing

Instructions:

Cast on 80 (110) sts.
Row 1: (WS). Knit.
Row 2: Knit.
Row 3: K, increase 18 (24) sts evenly across, 98 (134) sts.

🛑 Proceed in pattern as follows:
Row 1: (RS) Knit.
Row 2 and even rows: K3, purl to last 3 sts, k3.
Row 3: K4, *C6B, k6, C6F, repeat from * to last 4 sts. K4.
Row 5, 7, and 9: Knit.
Row 11: K7, C6F, C6B, * K6, C6F, C6B. Repeat from * to last 7 sts. K7.
Row 13 and 15: Knit.
Row 16: As 2nd row.
These 16 rows form pattern.
Continue in pattern until afghan measures approximately 39 (56)", ending on a 14th row of pattern.
Next row: (RS) K, decrease 18 (24) sts evenly across, 80 (110) sts.

K 2 rows. Bind off knitwise (WS).

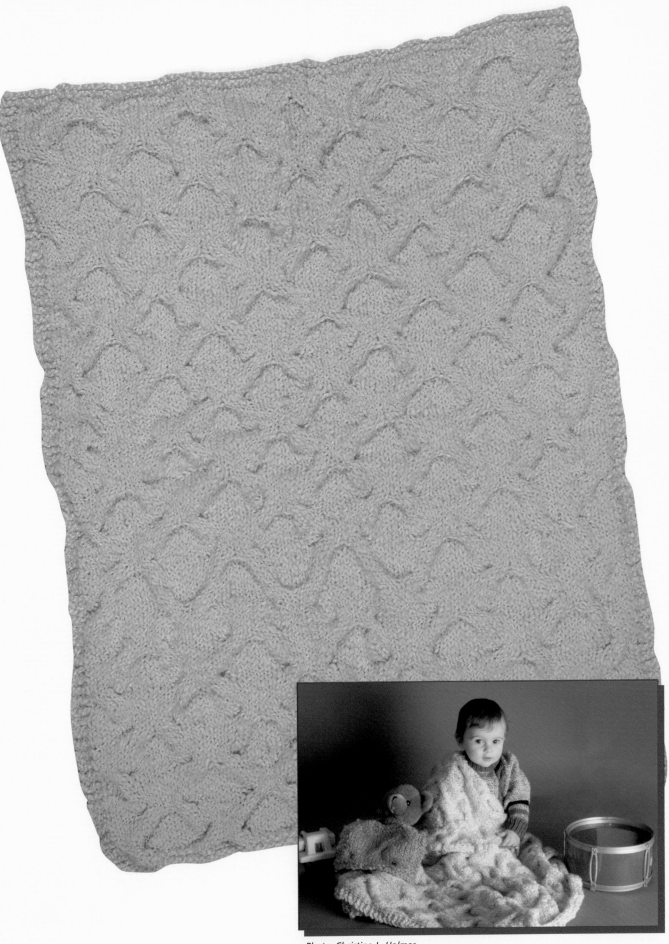

Photo: Christina L. Holmes

Grow-As-You-Go Diagonal Baby Afghan

Designed by Mary Colucci

Knitting on the diagonal is great fun. And as its name suggests, stitches have a diagonal slant. For our baby blanket, we started with a few stitches, increased until the knitted fabric was the length we liked and then we started decreasing a stitch every row, creating a square blanket. We did not have a formal pattern or gauge when we started. We simply combined yarn colors we liked and experimented with needle sizes until we got the "look" that we liked. Experiment with different yarns and sizes, too.

▽ Diagonal knitting is also a wonderful way to create shawls, and you don't have to decrease. Continue increasing until the triangle is a comfortable size for draping/wrapping around your shoulders and bind off. Also, try increasing on the first stitch instead of the second stitch of each row.

Size:

Approximately 36" square

Gauge:

With four strands of yarn and size 17 needles, 2 sts = 1"
To ensure proper size, take time to check your gauge.

Instructions:

NOTE: Blanket is knitted in stockinette stitch, holding one strand of each of the four yarn colors together at the same time.

With four strands of yarn, cast on three stitches.
Row 1: K1, increase 1 in next st, k1.
Row 2: P1, increase 1 st in 2nd st, p2.
Row 3: K1, increase 1 in next st, k3.
Row 4: P1, increase 1 in next st, p4.

MATERIALS:

❖ Caron's *Simply Soft*® (acrylic, 6 oz/300 yd skein)
  Orchid (#9717)
  Sage (#9705)
  Bone (#9703)
  Victorian Rose (#9721)
  —2 skeins of each color

❖ Size 17 circular needles, 24", or size to obtain gauge

❖ Size N/9 crochet hook (optional, see Finishing)

❖ Yarn or tapestry needle for finishing

Continue alternating k rows with p rows and increasing in the second st on each row until knitting measures 36" (or the length desired) along one edge.

Maintaining St st pattern (alternating k rows with p rows), begin decreasing one st in the 2nd st of every row until only 3 sts remain. Bind off.

Finishing:

The increases in diagonal knitting form a natural chain stitch and because the blanket is knitted in Stockinette stitch the edges roll in gently. If you like the look of the edges, no further finishing is necessary; simply weave in the yarn ends. We opted to crochet rows of loose slipstitch using two strands of the same color yarn for a border. (A single crochet border also would be attractive.)

Photo: Christina L. Holmes

Handy Mitten Scarf

Designed by Mary Colucci

Remember when your mother pinned your mittens to your sleeve so you wouldn't lose them? Well, here's a quick project idea that solves that age-old dilemma—the mitten scarf. Create warm "mittens" by simply turning up the ends of a scarf. Try this in your child's favorite colors or school colors. And, if you like the idea, make one for yourself, adjusting the length and amount of yarn.

Size:

Approximately 5½" wide and 52" long with 4½" "mitten" pockets

Gauge:

In garter stitch using two strands of yarn and size 13 needles,
   2½ sts = 1" 9 rows = 2"
To ensure proper sizing, take time to check gauge.

Instructions:

▽ **NOTE:** The scarf is made holding two strands of yarn held together throughout. When you need two strands and are knitting with one color and one skein of yarn, pull an end from the outside of the skein and an end from the inside of the skein. (The inside end can be tricky to find, but keep poking around, pulling out small amounts of yarn, until you do.)

When changing yarn colors every two or three rows, as you will here, you do not have to cut your yarn; simply carry the strands you are not using along the side edge. If the stripes are wider, it is better to cut the yarn, leaving approximately a 6" tail, which you can later weave in, and pick up the new yarn color.

MATERIALS:

* Caron *Simply Soft*® (acrylic, 6 oz/300 yd skein)
  White (#9701), Color A—1 skein
  Red Violet (#9718), Color B—1 skein
  Royale (#9713), Color C—1 skein
  Green (#9728), Color D—1 skein

* Size 13/9mm knitting needles, or size to obtain gauge

* Size 9/N crochet hook

* Yarn or tapestry needle for finishing

Cast on 15 sts. Knit all sts, changing colors as follows:
With B, k 27 rows.
With C, k 20 rows.
With A, k 10 rows.
One strand each of C and D, k 2 rows.
With A, k 2 rows.
With B, k 2 rows.
With A, k 6 rows.

With C, k 6 rows.
With D, k 6 rows.
With A, k 12 rows.
With B, k 20 rows.
With A, k 2 rows.
With D, k 22 rows.
With C, k 22 rows.
With A, k 2 rows.
With B, k 20 rows.
With A, k12 rows.

With D, k 6 rows.
With C, k 6 rows.
With A, k 6 rows.
With B, k 2 rows.
With A, k 2 rows.
One strand each of C and D, k 2 rows.
With A, k 10 rows.
With C, k 20 rows.
With B, k 27 rows.

Photo: Christina L. Holmes

Finishing:

With the WS facing you, at either end of the scarf, fold the bottom edge of the scarf up to the end of the first Color B stripe (approximately 4½"). Sew the side edges, creating a pocket. Turn the pocket inside out so it is on the right side of the scarf. With the crochet hook and holding a strand of A, B, C, and D together, crochet the edges with a very loose slipstitch or single crochet for a neat finish.

CHAPTER 9

HOW TO STITCH IT (AND FIX IT)

Following are instructions for most of the basic stitches used throughout this book as a handy quick-reference and "refresher" guide (you can't remember everything when you're living life in the fast lane!). These instructions are given for right-handed knitters; left-handers must substitute the word "right" for "left" and vice versa, in the instructions (and if you hold the instructions up to a mirror, they will be reversed to show the "left-handed" view). **NOTE:** We've used blue for the right-hand needle and red for the left-hand needle.

Casting On

This is the foundation row for your stitches. There are different methods of "casting on," but one of the most common—and simplest—is the double cast-on, or "long-tail" cast-on method.

First, measure off a length of yarn, allotting at least 1" for each stitch you will cast on. THIS IS IMPORTANT: Many knitters find they run out of yarn before they can cast on the required number of stitches, which is a big time-waster, particularly for those of us living in the fast lane! Be generous in leaving the "long tail" when you're casting on.

First, make a slip knot by forming a pretzel shape with the yarn, then slip your needle into the right loop of the "pretzel" as shown in Diagram 1.

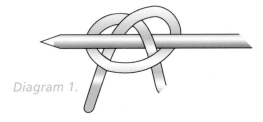

Diagram 1.

To tighten the knot, pull down on both ends of the yarn as in Diagram 2. Now you have one cast-on stitch on your needle.

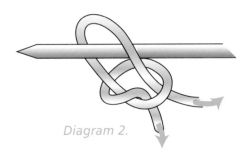

Diagram 2.

For the rest of your cast-on stitches, hold the needle with that first stitch on it in your right hand. Hold the yarn in your left hand, as shown in Diagram 3, with the short end of the yarn draped over the thumb, the yarn from the ball over your index finger, and the yarn ends held in your left palm with the other three fingers (or two fingers if it's more comfortable).

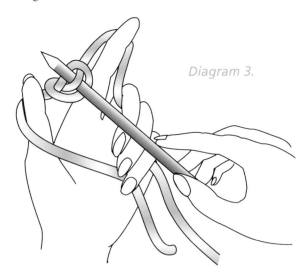

Diagram 3.

Insert the tip of your needle under the yarn on the left thumb from front to back, then over and under the strand on your left index finger, as in Diagrams 4, 5 and 6.

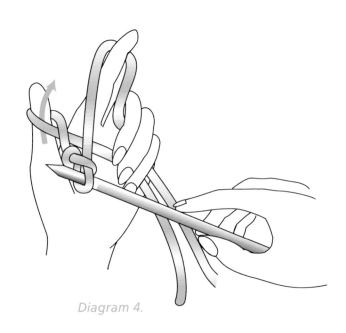

Diagram 4.

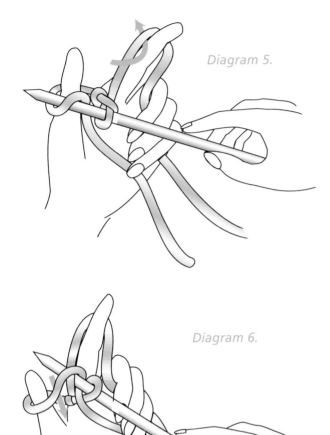

Diagram 5.

Diagram 6.

Draw this loop back through the loop on your thumb, as in Diagram 7, drop the loop on your thumb and pull the short (loose) end of the yarn to tighten the new stitch on the needle.

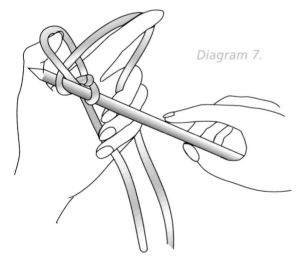

Diagram 7.

Repeat this method for each cast-on stitch required.

Knit Stitch (abbreviated as k)

Now you're ready to start knitting! Your left hand will hold the needle with the cast-on stitches, and your right hand will hold the yarn coming from the skein as in Diagram 8. The goal is to create an even tension with the yarn, so your stitches aren't too tight or too loose.

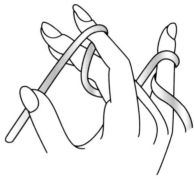

Diagram 8.

Be sure to make your stitches over the full roundness of the needle, not just the points, or your stitches will be much too tight.

Holding the needle with the cast-on stitches in your left hand, insert the right needle into the front of the first stitch, from front to back, as in Diagram 9. The right needle will be under the left one. **NOTE:** When you're doing a knit stitch, the yarn from the skein should be in BACK of the needles and your work.

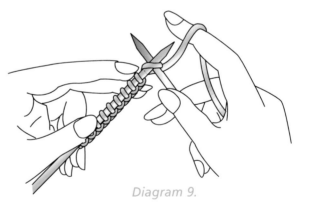

Diagram 9.

Bring the yarn from the skein under and over the right needle, from back to front, so it lies between the two needles, as in Diagram 10. Then bring the right needle with the yarn back through the stitch on the left needle, moving back to front, as in Diagram 11.

Now that you have the new stitch on the right needle, the next step is to slip the old stitch off the left one, by pulling it up and over the point of the left needle, as shown in Diagrams 12 and 13.

When you've repeated these steps to the end of your row, beginners should count their stitches to catch mistakes early on. Now, switch needles, so the needle full of stitches is back in your left hand, and you're ready to start another row.

To start the next row of knit stitch, insert your needle into the first stitch as shown in Diagram 14, and proceed as in Diagram 15.

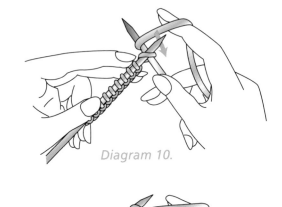

Diagram 10.

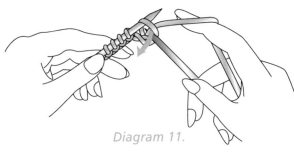

Diagram 11.

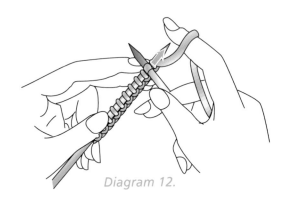

Diagram 12.

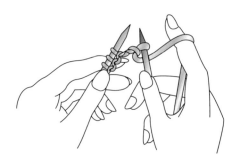

Diagram 13.

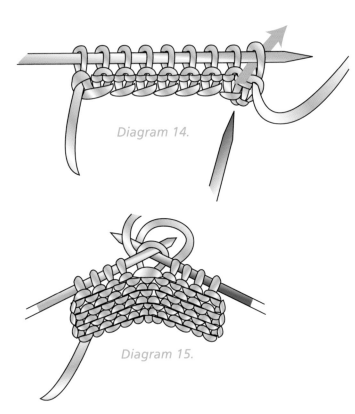

Diagram 14.

Diagram 15.

Garter Stitch (abbreviated as garter st)

When you knit every row, you're creating the garter stitch pattern, as shown in Diagram 16. The garter stitch has a bumpy texture, looks the same on both sides, and won't curl on the edges as will Stockinette stitch.

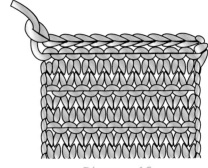

Diagram 16.

Each ridge you see in garter stitch equals two rows of knitting.

Purl Stitch (abbreviated as p)

A purl stitch is the reverse of a knit stitch—if you make a knit stitch and turn it around, the back looks like a purl stitch. The combination of knit and purl stitches is what creates the Stockinette stitch pattern (alternate rows of knit and purl) and a host of others. Remember when doing a purl stitch to keep your yarn from the skein positioned in FRONT of your needles and your work.

With your needle of cast-on stitches in your left hand, insert the right needle into the first stitch from right to left (back to front), so that your right needle is on top of the left needle, as in Diagram 17. Wrap the yarn around the right needle from right to left around the right needle, as shown in Diagram 18.

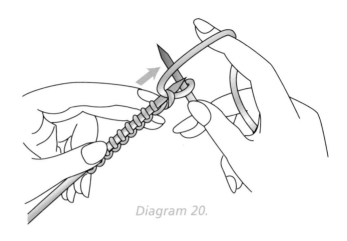

Diagram 20.

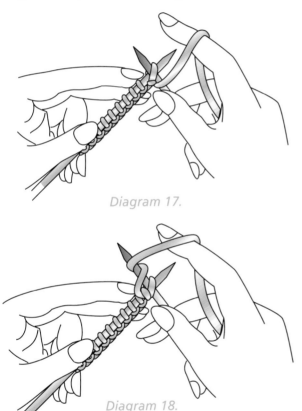

Diagram 17.

Diagram 18.

Slide the right needle with the yarn down through the stitch on the left needle, moving from front to back through the stitch, as shown in Diagram 19, then slide the old stitch off the needle, as in Diagram 20.

Diagram 19.

Stockinette Stitch (abbreviated as St st)

Stockinette stitch is created by knitting one row, purling the second, and continuing to alternate knit and purl rows throughout. In Stockinette stitch, you will always be knitting on a right-side row and purling on the wrong side row, so remember to bring the yarn to the back and front of your work as required. See Diagram 21.

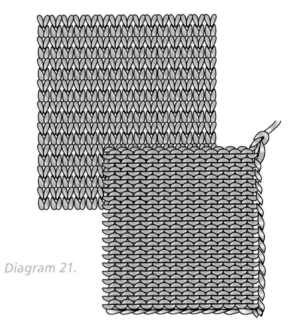

Diagram 21.

NOTE: Stockinette stitch is the stitch that will always roll at the edges. To counteract that, a pattern will often call for knitting the first one, two, or even three stitches of every purl row to create a "selvedge" (or "selvage") edge to stabilize the fabric and enable easier and neater assembly.

Reverse stockinette stitch is simply the "wrong" (purl) side of stockinette stitch used as the right side of your work.

Increasing (abbreviated as inc)

Increasing, or adding a stitch to make your piece wider, can be done by several methods, but the easiest is generally accepted to be knitting two stitches in one. To increase in a knit stitch, knit the stitch as you normally would, but DO NOT slip it off the left needle, as in Diagram 22.

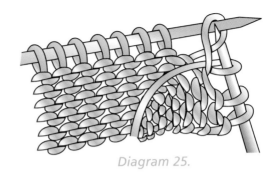

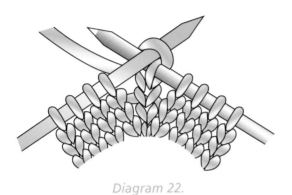

Diagram 22.

Now you will put your right needle into the stitch again, inserting it into the back of the stitch, as in Diagram 23.

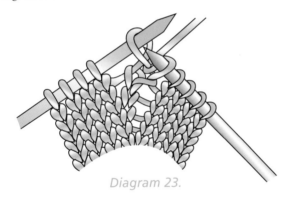

Diagram 23.

Wrap the yarn around the needle as you normally would for a knit stitch and draw through another stitch. Slip the old stitch off the left needle.

To increase in a purl stitch, purl that stitch as you normally would, but DO NOT slip it off the left needle. Then put the right needle into the BACK of the stitch, purl in that same stitch, and slip the stitch off the left needle as in Diagrams 24 and 25.

Diagram 24.

Diagram 25.

Decreasing (abbreviated as dec)

Probably the simplest way to decrease (to narrow your garment) is to knit or purl two stitches together (abbreviated as k2tog or p2tog) by inserting the needle into two stitches at the same time.

To knit two stitches together, insert the tip of the right needle into the front of the second stitch on the left needle, then through the first stitch, from left to right, as in Diagram 26, then knit the two stitches in the usual way, as if they were one stitch, as in Diagram 27.

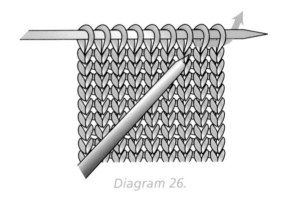

Diagram 26.

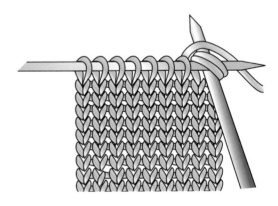

Diagram 27.

Decreasing in a purl row is done by inserting the right needle into two stitches at once, then purling them as if they were one stitch, creating a diagonal slant to the right, as in Diagram 28.

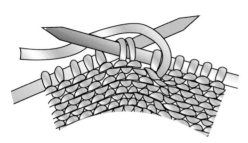

Diagram 28.

Slip, Knit and Pass Decrease Method
(abbreviated as SKP or sl 1, k 1, psso)

Depending on where a decrease is being worked on a garment, the instructions may call for this three-step method of decreasing to create a left diagonal slant.

First, slip a stitch from the left needle to the right needle knitwise, WITHOUT WORKING IT. (Just insert the right needle into the stitch and slip it off the left needle, as in Diagram 29.)

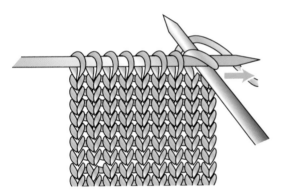

Diagram 29.

Now, knit the next stitch, so you have two stitches on the right needle, as in Diagram 30.

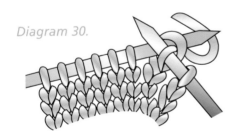

Diagram 30.

Now you'll use your left needle to "pass" the slipped stitch back over the knitted stitch and off the end of the right needle, by putting the left needle into the front of the slipped stitch and lifting it over the knitted stitch, as shown in Diagram 31. You've now decreased one stitch.

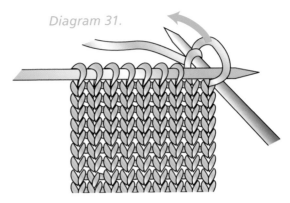

Diagram 31.

Binding Off

Patterns will sometimes tell you what method of binding off they want you to use. The following is a simple method that can be done on a knit or purl row. (Always bind off a row in the same stitch in which it was worked unless the pattern specifies otherwise.) Always bind off loosely, so the shape of the piece is not distorted and it remains flexible for ease of fit. Use larger needles for binding off if you find your bind off too tight.

Knit the first two stitches of the row. With the point of your left needle, lift up the first stitch and pull it over the second stitch as in Diagram 32, and off the right needle.

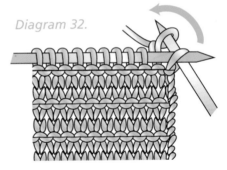

Diagram 32.

Now you'll have one stitch bound off and one stitch remaining on your right needle. Continue to work as before, knitting the next stitch and lifting the first stitch over the second and off the needle. At the end of the row, you'll be left with one stitch on your right needle. Leaving at least a 6" tail, cut the yarn and pull the end through the stitch using the tip of your right needle. Pull it tight to secure, as in Diagram 33.

Diagram 33.

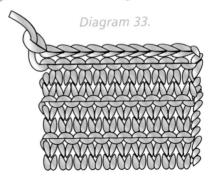

Joining Yarn

When you need to start a new skein or change colors, always do it at the beginning of a row if possible, leaving a 6" tail on the new yarn. With the new yarn, make a slip knot around the old yarn, as in Diagram 34, and continue working the next row. After a few stitches, tighten up the stitches at the beginning of the joining row and tie a temporary knot.

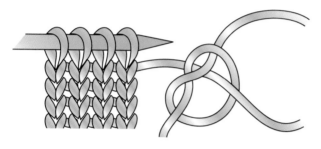

Diagram 34.

When you've finished your piece, go back and undo the knots, and weave in the ends for about 3".

There may be times when you run out of yarn in the middle of a row. If this happens, leave a 3" tail of the old yarn, wrap the new yarn around the right needle and continue working, as in Diagrams 35 and 36. Tie a knot and later weave in the ends to prevent holes and raveling. Remember, however, this is not the preferred way to join yarn.

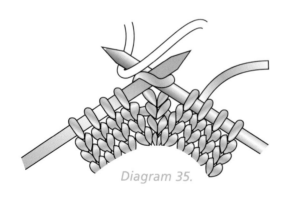

Diagram 35.

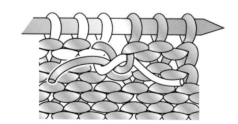

Diagram 36.

Ribbing Stitches

Several projects in this book call for ribbing on sleeves, waistbands or collars. This is simply a combination of knit and purl stitches, often just alternating knit and purl stitches across the row, as in the familiar "knit 1, purl 1" shown in Diagram 37. You'll usually find the ribbing stitch worked on a smaller needle than the body of the garment, for a snugger, but elastic fit. You'll always knit the knit stitches and purl the purl stitches on top of the ones in the row on which you're working.

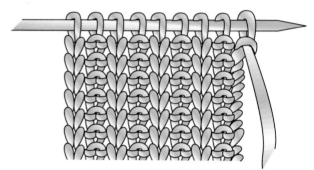

Diagram 37.

NOTE: It's important when working a ribbing stitch to remember to bring your yarn to the front when working the purl stitch and to the back when working the knit stitch.

Cables

A cable stitch is made by twisting or crossing a set of stitches over or under another group of stitches in the same row, and is accomplished with the use of a curved needle, called a cable stitch needle. You are going to put the stitches to be crossed onto the cable needle, according to the pattern instructions, knit the next group of stitches, then slip the stitches from the cable needle back onto the left needle and knit those stitches. The direction in which the cable twists depends on whether you cross the stitches in the front or back of your work. When you cross the stitches in front of your work, the cable will twist or spiral to the left; when you cross them in back of your work, you will have a "right-twist" cable.

The diagrams here show a left-twist cable:

In Diagram 38, our cable will consist of 6 stitches—3 in each half of the "twist"—twisted every few rows according to the pattern directions. First, place the stitches to be twisted on a cable needle as shown.

Then, knit the next group of stitches, as in Diagram 39.

The next step is to slip the stitches off the cable needle onto the left needle and work those stitches, as in Diagram 40.

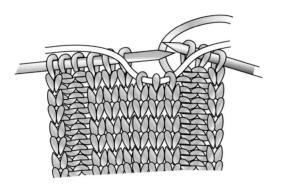

Diagram 38.

Diagram 39.

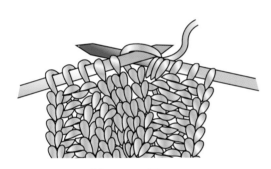

Diagram 40.

Continue as per pattern instructions to create your cable, as in Diagram 41.

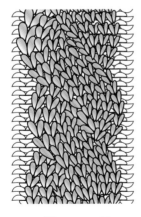

Diagram 41.

Yarn Over (abbreviated yo)

Yarn over means looping the yarn over the needle to create a "hole" or space in working lacy or decorative patterns and buttonholes.

Start by laying the yarn across the top of the needle.

These diagrams show a yarn over between knit stitches, then between purl stitches (less commonly used).

First, bring the yarn under to right needle to the front of your work, then over the right needle to the back, as in Diagram 42. Now you can knit the next stitch.

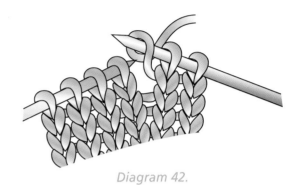

Diagram 42.

To do a yarn over between purl stitches, the yarn would be brought over the right needle to the back of the work, then under the right needle and to the front, as in Diagram 43.

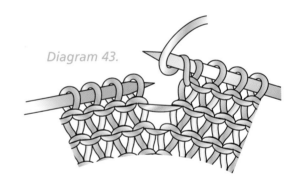

Diagram 43.

Slip Stitch (abbreviated sl st)

When a pattern says to slip a stitch, you simply transfer it from the left needle to the right needle without knitting or purling. Frequently, a pattern will say slip a stitch "knitwise" or "purlwise" which means you insert the right needle into the first stitch on the left needle as it if you were going to knit or purl and transfer it to the right needle.

Oops! Correcting Mistakes

We can't believe it—you made a mistake! Just kidding—even experienced knitters make mistakes, whether it's dropping a stitch or making an error in the number or type of stitches in a row. Here are some simple methods to help you get back on track.

A dropped stitch will look like Diagram 44, with the "bars" above it.

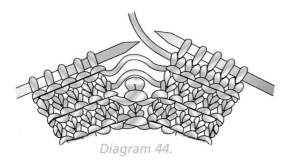
Diagram 44.

You want to pull the bar of the dropped stitch through these loops, recreating a stitch, and you want the new stitch to look just like all the others in that row.

You have two choices when you drop a stitch: unravel your knitting until you get to the dropped stitch row, as in Diagram 45; or, if there are not too many rows involved, use a crochet hook to pick it up. How you pick it up can be a little tricky, but here's an easy way to remember what to do.

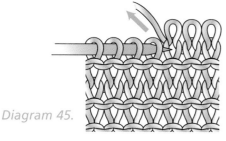
Diagram 45.

Picking Up a Dropped Stitch

First, you'll have to determine if the dropped stitch was a knit or purl stitch, then use the appropriate method to pick it up. If the stitches in the row above the dropped stitch are "flat" (knit stitches) as shown in

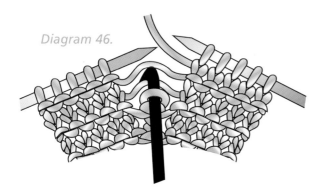
Diagram 46.

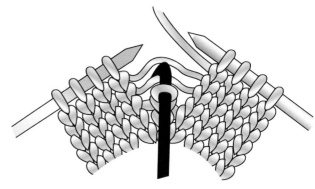
Diagram 47.

Diagram 46 or 47, pull the crochet hook into the dropped stitch from front to back (the bar will be in the back), hook onto the bar and pull the strand through the loop on the hook.

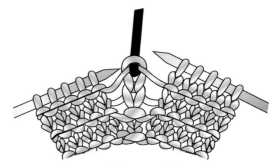
Diagram 48.

If, however, the stitches in the row above are "bumpy" (purl), as in Diagram 48, insert the crochet hook into the dropped loop from back to front, with the loose strand of the row above in FRONT of the dropped loop.

Continue until you come up to the working row, and put the stitch back on the left needle, taking care to insert the needle through the front of the stitch, so it's not twisted as you continue to work.

Correcting Twisted Stitches

Twisted stitches are especially apparent (need we say "glaring?") when you're working with bulky yarns or holding more than one strand together, as in Diagram 49, which shows twisted stitches in a knit row.

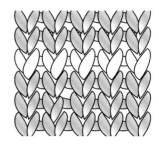
Diagram 49.

You may have inserted your needle into the back of the stitch instead of the front when you were working stockinette stitch, or put the yarn over the needles incorrectly, or picked up a stitch the wrong way.

To correct a twisted stitch in a knit row, knit it through the back loop to correct it; in a purl row, purl it through the back loop.

Correcting Extra Stitches

It's all too easy to wind up with extra stitches on your needle, particularly when working with some of the "furry" yarns and multiple strands. Other than counting stitches as you go, one of the best ways to avoid this is to remember to keep the yarn UNDER the needle when moving it to the back to knit a stitch. Diagram 50 shows the INCORRECT method, and Diagram 51 shows the correct positioning of the yarn.

INCORRECT

Diagram 50.

CORRECT

Diagram 51.

In a row of purl stitches, keep the yarn at the front of the work and below the needle, as in Diagram 52.

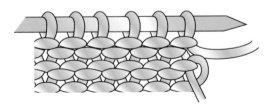

Diagram 52.

Finishing Stitches

Some patterns may specify the type of finishing stitches to use; others will let you use whatever method you're most comfortable with. Here are some common options. Whichever one you use, remember to keep it loose to allow for stretch and better fit, and always use matching yarn, unless otherwise specified.

Backstitch

A familiar stitch to embroiderers (and used in our Loop Trim Scarf to create the "border trim"), this stitch must be worked close to the edge of the pieces you are seaming together to avoid taking a deep seam that will be thick and bulky in your garment.

Place the pieces right sides together, than come up through the fabric at point A, make a stitch backwards, going down through point B, up at C, down at D, and so forth, as in Diagram 53.

Diagram 53.

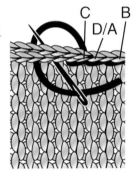

Overcast Stitch

Place right sides together and insert needle back to front, bringing the needle over the edge. Insert needle back to front again, catching only one or two strands from each edge, as in Diagram 54.

Diagram 54.

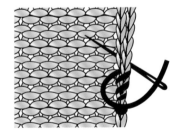

This is not considered an ideal stitch for garments, since it may not give you the smooth finish you'd like on the right side of a garment, but is good for non-wearables such as afghans or handbags.

Weaving (Invisible or "Mattress" Stitch)

Weaving is an almost invisible way to finish seams, particularly side seams. With right sides facing you and edges touching, pick up the bar between the first and second stitches on one side, then the bar between the first and second stitches on the other side. Continue working back and forth gently pulling yarn to close seam.

NOTE: Weaving is particularly good for shoulder seams and for setting in a sleeve into an armhole, as it allows you to ease and adjust for fit.

Crochet Seam Finishes

If you like to crochet, this is an easy one. Working with right sides together, matched row to row, attach a skein of yarn at the beginning of the seam. Insert the crochet hook into the outer loop of the first stitch at the top of the piece, go through to the bottom piece of fabric and pick up the corresponding outside loop. Pull your seaming yarn through the two loops of knitted fabric, for one slipstitch. You will have one loop on your hook. From this point on, you'll insert the hook into the outer loops of each of the two fabric pieces, and have three loops (one of the seaming yarn and two from the knitted pieces) on your hook. Wrap the seaming yarn over the hook and draw through all three loops as in Diagrams 56 and 57.

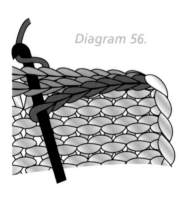

Diagram 56.

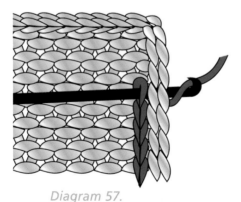

Diagram 57.

Picking Up Stitches

Several of the patterns in this book require you to "pick up stitches" as you work. Pick up stitches with the right side facing you, so the resulting ridge will be on the wrong side of your work (unless the pattern specifies otherwise).

Use the needles and yarn you are going to be continuing to work in to pick up the stitches. Insert your needle from front to back under two strands and the edge of the piece, as in Diagram 58.

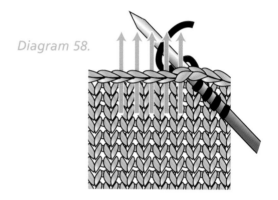

Diagram 58.

Wrap the yarn around the needle as if you were going to knit a stitch, then bring the needle back through the stitch to the right side, which will give you a stitch on the needle, as in Diagram 59.

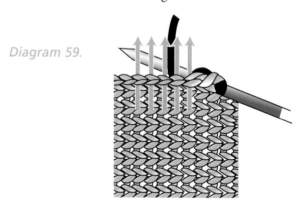

Diagram 59.

Keep working along the edge as directed.

Crochet Stitches

Some of the patterns in this book use simple crochet stitches, in particular for finishing. We've already shown the slip stitch under the finishing techniques, but here are some others you'll run across.

Chain (abbreviated as ch)

Yarn over the hook, pull through loop on hook, as in Diagram 60.

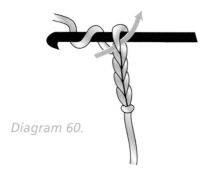

Diagram 60.

Single Crochet (abbreviated as sc)

Insert your hook in the stitch, wrap yarn over the hook, pull the yarn through the stitch, wrap the yarn over the hook again, and pull the yarn through both loops on the hook, as in Diagram 61.

Diagram 61.

Double Crochet (abbreviated as dc)

On top of your chain stitch (or along the edge of a knitted piece that serves as a foundation), wrap yarn over the hook, insert the hook from front to back into the fourth chain or stitch from the hook, as in Diagrams 62 and 63.

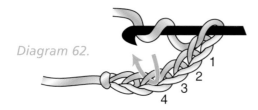

Diagram 62.

Diagram 63.

Yarn over and draw that loop through the first loop on the chain, leaving three loops on the hook, as in Diagram 64.

Diagram 64.

Yarn over again and draw that loop through the two loops on the hook, leaving two loops on the hook, as shown in Diagram 65.

Diagram 65.

Yarn over and pull that loop through two loops on the hook, leaving one loop on the hook, one double crochet completed, as in Diagram 66.

Diagram 66.

Reverse Single Crochet
(abbreviated as Rsc)

This stitch produces a cording effect that many knitters love. You may see it described as "crab stitch," "shrimp stitch" or "corded stitch." It's worked with the right side of the fabric facing you but in the opposite direction in which you would normally work (right handers work left to right). Pay attention to the direction in which the crochet hook points.

Beginning at the opposite end from where you'd normally start, right side facing you and one loop on the crochet hook, insert the hook head downward into the first stitch. Draw up one loop of yarn through the stitch for two loops on the hook. See Diagrams 67 and 68.

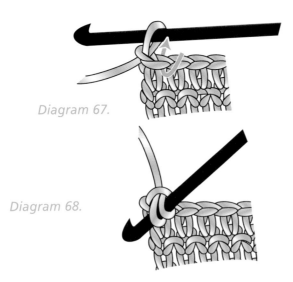

Diagram 67.

Diagram 68.

Now turn the head of the hook facing downward, wrap the yarn over the hook and pull it through the two loops on the hook (as in Diagrm 69). You have completed one reverse single crochet. Continue across row as in Diagram 70.

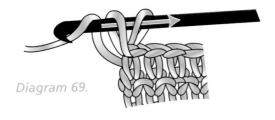

Diagram 69.

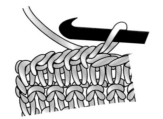

Diagram 70.

Making Fringe

Some of the items in this book call for fringe. Using a piece of cardboard cut to the desired length, wind several strands around it, secure with tie, and cut at bottom, as in Diagram 71 and 72. If you prefer, just measure out strands to twice the length of the desired fringe.

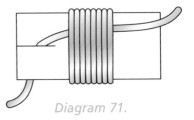

Diagram 71.

Diagram 72.

With the fringe folded in half over the crochet hook, pull the strands through the edge of your knitted piece and pull the yarn through the loop, as in Diagram 73.

Diagram 73.

Space out tassels at desired intervals as shown in Diagram 74.

Diagram 74.

Appendix

Abbreviations & Commonly Used Terms*

beg	beginning
BO	bind off
CC	contrasting color
dec	decrease
dpn	double pointed needle
EOR	every other row
inc	increase
in(s) or "	inches
k	knit
k2tog	knit two (stitches) together
MC	main color
mm	millimeter
oz(s)	ounce(s)
p	purl
psso	pass slipped stitch(es) over
p2tog	purl two stitch(es) together
RS	right side
sl	slip
ssk	slip, slip, knit
st(s)	stitch(es)
St st	stockinette stitch
WS	wrong side
yo	yarn over
* *	repeat directions between * * as many times as indicated

*We only list abbreviations used in this book. There are others commonly used in commercial patterns. Always check the pattern key before you begin your knitting.

Pattern Lingo

"work"
When reading patterns in this book and other resources, "work," "work even," "work across," or "work up" are commonly used terms. "Work" is just another way of saying, "keep on knitting." For instance, if the pattern says, "work across," continue following the pattern established and complete the row.

"knitwise" or "purlwise"
When you see these terms, they mean to insert your right needle into the next stitch on the left needle as if you were going to knit or purl. For instance, a pattern might say, "Slip the next stitch purlwise," which mean slip the next stitch as if you were going to purl that stitch but you don't.

"back loop"
Knitting into the back loop of a stitch, sometimes abbreviated "tbl" (through the back loop), twists the stitch. If you are knitting, instead of putting the right needle through the front loop of the stitch on the left needle, insert it into the back loop as you normally would from the front to back and complete the new stitch as usual, drawing a loop through. To purl through the back loop, which is done in the "Cable Sweat Suit" in the *Hey Baby Chapter*, bring the right needle from the back to the front through the back loop of the stitch on the left needle and complete the stitch as usual.

Fast FAQs

I don't understand what the pattern is telling me to do.

Just don't understand pattern instructions? Here's what Evie always tells us and it works much of the time: "It's always easier with your knitting in front of you." Take out your needles and yarn and then try following the pattern instructions, one step at a time.

Why aren't the edges of my knitting straight?

Having trouble keeping the edges of your knitting straight? It can be tricky, especially when you use textured or dark-colored yarns, because stitches are difficult to see clearly. One of the most common errors is picking up an extra stitch at the end of the row. This usually happens when you bring the yarn over the needle. Check out the illustration in the Stitch Instructions, Diagrams 50 and 51. Count your stitches frequently. If you have added stitches, unravel your knitting to the row where the problem started.

Where did those extra stitches come from?

You counted your stitches and you have more than you should have. The edges look straight. Where did they come from? Another common mistake that adds unwanted stitches to your knitting is forgetting to drop the "old" stitch from the left needle after you have pulled up the loop of yarn forming the new stitch, or picking up the yarn between stitches and knitting it, creating a new stitch.

Fitting stitches on the needles: How much is too many?

There are no hard and fast rules about the length needle you should use, but you want your stitches to fit on the needle and slide easily without "popping off." When knitting bulky sweaters, using multiple strands of yarn or making afghans, you might want to consider using circular needles. Just like straight knitting needles, circulars come in different lengths.

When do you use circulars?

In addition to large projects, circulars are frequently used in this book for finishing necklines, where you are picking up stitches in a circle and which would be awkward to do with straight needles.

How do you work with circular needles?

You can use circular needles just like straight needles, knitting back and forth, or you can knit in the round, creating a tubular piece of knitting. To use circular needles like straight needles, you knit your stitches from the left needle to the right. At the end of the row, you turn your work so that the yarn end is in your left hand. If you don't turn your work at the end of the row, and just keep going, you'll knit a tube. When knitting in the round, the right side of fabric always faces you. Accordingly, when working a Stockinette stitch, knit all the stitches on every round. When working a garter stitch, alternate knit and purl rows.

Working with two or more strands of yarn sounds complicated.

There's nothing complicated in multiple-strand knitting. When a pattern says to knit using two or more strands of yarn, hold them together and knit them as if they were one strand. You do not want to wind the different colors or yarns into one ball; simply pull a thread from each skein or ball. Occasionally, you will have to untwist the yarns to keep them flat and untangled. There are more tips on working with multiple strands of yarn in the "Tips on working with textured yarns" section in this chapter.

Do the same needle sizes differ?

Yes, there are subtle differences in needle sizing between manufacturers, which is another reason to always check your gauge.

Are the same knitting abbreviations used around the world?

No, there are variations. Always consider the source of your project pattern and check the abbreviation key.

How do I start a new skein of yarn in the middle of a project?

Oops! You ran out of yarn and have to start a new skein. It's best to start a new skein at the beginning of a row because it is easier to work in the ends when you finish the project. See Stitch Instructions, Diagrams 34-36. Simply drop the yarn you had been working with and start knitting with yarn from the new skein. Some people find it is easier to tie a loose knot with the yarn ends. When they finish the project, they untie the knot and work in the ends.

I want to change the size of a pattern. Can I do it?

If you want to make a sweater larger or smaller than the sizes provided, we really recommend that you ask an expert knitter to assist you. Adjusting the shaping can be done but it's complicated and some patterns just cannot be changed. Your best bet is always to find a pattern that is written in your size range.

Knots: Why can't I make them?

The experts say, "No knots," for three very good reasons:

1. Knots inevitably "pop" through to the front of your project,
2. They leave bumps in your knitting, and
3. They come out!

How do I change yarn color for horizontal stripe patterns?

When you are changing yarn colors to create a horizontal stripe pattern, you will often cut off one yarn color, leaving a 6" end, and pick up the new color and continue knitting. If a yarn color is repeated every other row or every two rows, you can "carry" the yarn color not being used along the side of your work. When you finish the stripe of one color, simply pick up the strand of the other color and begin knitting.

Why are there holes in my knitting?

You might have dropped a stitch, in which case, you should check out Diagrams 44-48 in the Stitch Instructions, which show how to pick up dropped stitches.

Can I pull the yarn end from the center of the skein?

It's preferable to pull yarn from the inside of the yarn skein or ball rather than use the outside end. The skein stays neater and the yarn is less likely to get tangled. However, finding that inside end can be tricky. There are instructions on some skeins but on others you just have to stick two fingers into the center of the skein and fish around. Usually, you'll pull out a wad of yarn but eventually you'll find the end.

My stitches are tight stitches. I can hardly move them across the needle.

If your stitches are barely moving along the needle, you need to loosen up and not pull the yarn so tight. As you become more comfortable holding the needles, your tension will loosen up. If you tighten your stitch on the shaft of the needle rather than on the point, it will help to ease your tight tension. Tight tension can be a special problem when you cast on because you want that row to be stretchy and flexible. You'll probably find that you will have to switch to a larger-size needle to obtain the necessary gauge for your project (see section on Gauge in this chapter).

My stitches are too loose. What can I do to make them look even?

If your stitches are too loose, you need to focus on pulling the yarn tighter as you are making your stitches. Sometimes it is easy to "stretch" your stitches, which makes them look larger and misshapen. To prevent stretching, position the stitches as close to the edge of your needle as possible so you do not have to pull the yarn. Practice making the stitch loops uniform on the needle. Practice is the best thing.

Help! The edges of my knitting are curling.

Certain stitches, such as stockinette (alternately knitting one row and purling one row), almost always will curl in, which can be an attractive edging. However, if you hate that look, consider adding two knit stitches at the beginning and end of every row. If you have already completed your project, you can crochet a border. It will help to flatten the knitting, but you'll have to do several rows to really straighten it out and it might not flatten out completely.

What's a "ridge" in garter stitch?

Two rows of knitting make a ridge. For more details on garter stitch, see the Stitch Instructions.

Cast on: How much yarn will I need for my tail so I don't run out before I finish casting on?

If you use the double cast-on or long tail method, figure on one inch of yarn for every one stitch as a general rule, however, bulky yarns or multi-stranded work may require more. Be generous!

The yarn I'm using is in a hank and I'm finding it difficult to work with.

Several of the yarns mentioned in this book come in hanks. To prevent tangles, it is helpful to wind the hank into a ball before you start your project. Untwist the hank and find one end. (It's helpful to have someone hold the hank while you wind it or slip it over the back of a chair.) Wind the yarn around your fingers several times, then slip the yarn off your fingers, turn slightly and roll several more times over your fingers and continue until all the yarn is wound. This process prevents you from pulling the yarn too tightly and stretching it.

Here's a general rule for picking up stitches that are not on a holder. If you are picking up along a horizontal or bound off edge, pick up one stitch in each stitch. For stitches along a vertical edge, pick up 3 stitches for every four rows. And for a diagonal, pick up one stitch per stitch or row. But when all is said and done, it's really what looks best to you that's the rule. It's ok to pick up fewer stitches if you are pleased with the finished look.

Resource List

Following is a list of suppliers of yarns used in this book.

Bernat Yarns
P.O. Box 40
Listowell, Ont.
Canada, N4W 3H3
P.O. Box 435
Lockport, NY 14094
www.bernat.com

Berroco, Inc.
14 Elmdale Rd.
Uxbridge, MA 01569-0367
www.berroco.com

Caron International
1481 W. 2nd St.
P.O. Box 222
Washington, NC 27889
www.caron.com

Coats & Clark
(Red Heart Yarns)
8 Shelter Drive
Greer, SC 29650
www.coatsandclark.com

The Great Adirondack Yarn Co.
950 Co. Hwy. 125
Amsterdam, NY 12010

Lion Brand Yarn Co.
34 W. 15th St.
New York, NY 10011
www.lionbrand.com

Muench Yarns
(distributors of Horstia)
285 Bel Marin Keys Blvd.
Unit J
Novato, CA 94949-5724

Reynolds Yarns
Division of JCA, Inc.
35 Scales Lane
Townsend, MA 01469

Skacel Collection (Mondial Yarns)
P.O. Box 88110
Seattle, WA 98138-2110
www.skacelknitting.com

Unique Kolours
(Colinette Hand Dyed Yarns)
1428 Oak Lane
Downingtown, PA 19335
www.uniquekolours.com

For information on learning how to knit or crochet, Warm Up America!, special events, guilds, or just connecting with other knitters, log on to **www.knitandcrochet.com** at the Craft Yarn Council of America Web site.